THE HOUSE FLIPPING

ANSWERBOOK

Practical Answers to More Than 125 Questions on How to Find, Fix, and Sell Houses for Profit

DENISE L. EVANS,
ATTORNEY AT LAW

SPHINX® PUBLISHING
AN IMPRINT OF SOURCEBOOKS, INC.®
NAPERVILLE, ILLINOIS
www.SphinxLegal.com

First Edition, 2008

Published by: **Sphinx® Publishing, An Imprint of Sourcebooks, Inc.®**

Naperville Office
P.O. Box 4410
Naperville, Illinois 60567-4410
630-961-3900
Fax: 630-961-2168
www.sourcebooks.com
www.SphinxLegal.com

This publication is designed to provide accurate and authoritative information in regard to the subject matter covered. It is sold with the understanding that the publisher is not engaged in rendering legal, accounting, or other professional service. If legal advice or other expert assistance is required, the services of a competent professional person should be sought.

From a Declaration of Principles Jointly Adopted by a Committee of the American Bar Association and a Committee of Publishers and Associations

This product is not a substitute for legal advice.

Disclaimer required by Texas statutes

Library of Congress Cataloging-in-Publication Data

Evans, Denise L.

The house flipping answer book : practical answers to the top 125 questions on how to find, fix, and sell houses for profit / by Denise L. Evans. -- 1st ed.

p. cm.

Includes bibliographical references and index.

ISBN 978-1-57248-648-5 (pbk. : alk. paper) 1. Real estate investment. 2. House buying. 3. House selling. 4. Real estate business. I. Title. II. Title: Sell houses for profit.

HD1382.5.E968 2008

332.63'240973--dc22

2007048788

Printed and bound in the United States of America.

CH — 10 9 8 7 6 5 4 3 2 1

Contents

Chapter 1

INTRODUCTION TO FLIPPING HOUSES

- What is flipping?
- Someone told me flipping is now illegal. Is that true?
- What kind of person will be successful at flipping?
- Is there more than one type of flip?
- Is it possible to flip even when the market is depressed?
- Can I flip houses like people do on the television shows?
- Can I flip my own house?
- Is there a flip for people who are afraid of power tools?
- Can I flip rental houses?
- Is it easy to flip vacant rental houses?
- How can I flip with no cash, no credit, and no power tools?
- I do not like fixing things up. Is there another kind of flip I can do?
- How does the option flip work?
- I read about people getting rich flipping condos. How does that work?
- Can I buy foreclosures as a type of flip?
- Is it possible to just find bargains, do nothing, and flip for a profit?
- What is the parcel flip?
- Can I make money finding flipping opportunities for other people?
- What are the risks associated with flipping?
- How do I get started in flipping?

What is flipping?

In real estate, *flipping* consists of gaining control of real estate for a short period of time with the intention of selling it to someone else at a profit. While this definition may seem fairly vague, that is because there are many different ways to flip property. You have probably noticed that this definition does not say, "buying and owning real estate for a short period of time..." You can successfully flip houses all day long and never take title to real estate, go through a closing, borrow money, have a silent partner, and never risk any of your own money. (See Chapter 4 on options for more information on this method of flipping.)

Someone told me flipping is now illegal. Is that true?

No, it is not true. You can find articles and blogs all over the Internet that say the same thing. It is just a case of people being sloppy about how they describe a problem.

The Federal Housing Administration (FHA) insures a lot of home mortgage loans. This allows the loans to be sold on the secondary market, which gives the lender the money it needs to make more loans. The FHA was concerned about widespread fraudulent practices in which partners would flip properties to each other, over and over, artificially inflating the price each time. No real money changed hands until the very end, when some lender got stuck with a $500,000 loan on a $150,000 house, and the FHA had to pay off on the insurance.

To put the brakes on that type of activity, the FHA issued rules saying it would not insure any home loan for a property that had been purchased and then resold within a ninety-day period. Also, if the property had been bought and resold within a six-month period, and the price doubled, FHA would require two appraisals before it would insure the loan. This makes it more difficult even for legitimate real estate investors to flip properties in some circumstances. There is nothing illegal about flipping, though.

What kind of person will be successful at flipping?

Anybody can be successful at flipping property because there are so many different ways to do it. You just need to match your personality, strengths, and limitations to the right style. The questions answered as follows will help you choose the strategy that is right for you. The ideal flipper has plenty of the following:

- cash;
- credit;
- time;
- discipline;
- knowledge;
- contacts;
- assistance; and,
- organizational skills.

Even if you give yourself an F on every single item on this list, you can still successfully flip property! Read the brief descriptions of flip strategies given in the next answer to find out which one works best for you.

Is there more than one type of flip?

There are many ways to flip property. Popular television shows spotlight *fixer-uppers*—diamonds in the rough needing only paint, carpet, counters, cabinet doors, appliances, landscaping, and the moving of a few walls. While it is true that the single-project, big-payoff flip falls into this category, this type of flip has the most risk and is the least realistic option for most people. On the other hand, it is really hard to make an interesting one-hour television show out of people making money simply by cleaning up dirty houses and selling them.

Here are some of the more popular flipping strategies. Some require no cash and no credit. Some have little risk, except the loss of a very small amount of money and your time.

1. *The television flip.* Buy a house, fix it up to increase its value by a lot, and sell it.

2. *The homeowner flip.* Buy a house as your personal residence, fix it up to increase its value, and sell it after two years. Singles can make up to a $250,000 profit and married couples can make up to a $500,000 profit, and pay no taxes on this profit at all under current tax law.

3. *The housekeeper flip.* Buy a house, clean it up to increase its value a little bit, and sell it.

4. *The market rent flip.* Buy a rental house with rents that are significantly below market rates, raise the rent, and sell it.

5. *The vacancy rate.* Buy a vacant rental house, put a tenant in place, and sell it.

6. *The tenant flip.* Rent a house on a lease with a purchase option, clean it up and perform minor repairs to increase

value moderately, and then sell your option (this flip technique requires little cash and no credit).

7. *The scrape flip.* Buy property with an ugly, barely usable building, bulldoze the building, and level the lot. Then, sell the vacant lot.

8. *The option flip.* Buy an *option* on a piece of property—you pay a small amount to hold the right to buy property but not the obligation to buy it—and then sell your option. (There is more detailed information on this type of flip in Chapter 4 on options.)

9. *The reservation flip.* Sign contracts to buy property in a booming market and then hope you can sell your contract to someone else, at a profit, before you have to be at the closing table with your purchase money. (It is called a *reservation flip* because this is usually done with reservations for condos under construction.)

10. *The foreclosure owner flip.* Buy property at below-market prices from sellers in economic difficulty and then resell. I include in this category reluctant owners, like banks that have already foreclosed on property. While a bank does not need the money to pay the electric bill, it is still in economic distress relative to the property because it has economic pressures to sell the property as quickly as possible to cut its losses.

11. *The under-market flip.* Buy or option property from owners

who seriously undervalue their property and then sell it.

12. *The parcel flip.* Buy large parcels of property and then break them up into smaller parcels that sell at a larger per-acre or per-square-foot price.

13. *The assemblage flip.* Option very small parcels of property that are all next to each other and then sell them all in one large parcel.

14. *The scout.* Find property for other people to flip and earn a flat fee or a minor percentage of the profit.

Is it possible to flip even when the market is depressed?

Absolutely you can still successfully flip houses even in a down market. You need to set your goals at a higher profit before you buy, so you will have a larger cushion in case the market continues downward. You might not make as much money as you originally expected, but you will not get hurt, either, if you plan your flip correctly.

Remember, in a depressed or downward trending market, many people still buy houses. There are buyers out there. As far as sellers go, many people will not be able to afford necessary repairs before selling their houses, giving you many opportunities for bargain purchases. Other sellers are facing foreclosure or similar matters that motivate them to sell cheaply.

Also, as more and more people face foreclosure or sell their homes to get out from under heavy mortgage payments, those same people must move somewhere else. Typically, they move into rental houses rather than apartments. You can buy a house, put a tenant in place, and then sell that rental house to an investor. Many people who lose or sell their homes do so, not because they could no longer afford the monthly payments, but because they got behind on their payments for some temporary problem and then cannot afford to catch up again. Those people are willing and able to pay relatively high rental rates, sometimes for the same home they used to own.

Can I flip houses like people do on the television shows?

I call this the *television flip*. It is fast paced, exciting, attracts a lot of cheerleaders, and results in huge profits. Remember though, most of television is about entertainment, not education. At least one house-flipping show has suffered widespread criticism when people learned that many of its segments were staged.

Do not get me wrong—the television flip opportunity exists, but you are not going to find seven pieces of property you can do this with during your first week in the business. Most beginners should stick to one of the other strategies listed previously, but they should still be ready to act if they find a house that seems right for a television flip.

The person who is an ideal candidate for the big investment of time that is necessary to hunt for, find, and successfully complete a television flip is someone who can spend more than forty hours a week on the venture, is very organized, and who can afford the inevitable delays that come with a big project. You will have to look at—and reject—a lot of houses before finding the right one. Organizational skills are important to help you sift through all that information and to manage the thousand details of a big renovation project. Finally, every large project has surprises, every surprise means some sort of a delay, and delays cost money. You must have the staying power to continue making mortgage payments two or three months longer than you may have intended and to pay for things not anticipated in your original budget.

Can I flip my own house?

The *homeowner flip* is the best type of flip for most people. You can take your time to make repairs and upgrades. Home mortgage interest rates are usually lower when you live in the house than commercial loan rates offered to flippers who do not use the property as their personal residence. You do not have to be terribly organized. And—a big plus—under tax laws in effect when this book was published, you can sell the house and make up to $250,000 in profit if you are single or $500,000 if you are married and pay absolutely no income taxes on the profit!

So, what does it take to do a successful homeowner flip? You absolutely, positively, must remember that your house is an investment. Even if you do not have children, buy in a good school district, since this will be something that potential buyers may be concerned with. Before you buy anything for the house or spend any money on improvements, ask yourself two questions: (1) Will this purchase increase the value enough to pay for itself? and, (2) Is this a matter of personal taste that might not appeal to everyone else? This is probably the most difficult part of doing a homeowner flip. When I made a conscious decision to flip one of my homes, it was really hard to tell myself that I could not have a gourmet kitchen no matter how much I wanted one because the market simply would not support it. I would not have been able to get my money back on that expense, so it was not worth spending the money. If you are the kind of person who can keep your mind on the goal and do without the little things along the way in order to get a larger payoff at the end, you will not have any trouble doing this kind of flip.

Is there a flip for people who are afraid of power tools?

Even if you are afraid of power tools, you can take advantage of the easiest flip of all—and the one most often overlooked by investors. It is called the *housekeeper flip*. A stunning number of people try to sell homes that look like fifty children just tore through the house. These houses will sit on the market forever, since very few people want to buy a new house and then clean up the mess. At some point, the owner probably just wants to get out, for almost any price. You can usually buy for 5%–10% below the market value, just because the house is dirty and messy! Sometimes the discount can be even greater.

While you will not make a huge profit on this type of flip, it is a way to make a small profit that is quick, painless, and worry free. If you are able to do four to six housekeeper flips a year, and make a $10,000 profit on each one, you can easily live comfortably on your income from the flips.

Can I flip rental houses?

You can flip rental houses in all the same ways you can flip a personal residence, plus there are some extra methods you can utilize. These additional strategies are as follows.

1. Buy at a purchase price based on a current rental rate that is significantly less than market rents for similar properties.

2. If the rent is too low based on other rents being charged in

the area, simply raise the rent, or make needed repairs or cosmetic improvements to justify a higher rent.

3. Sell at a sales price based on the new current rental rate that is equal to, or perhaps even slightly higher than, market rents for similar properties.

As you begin to research rents, you will find an amazing number of landlords who do not keep track of what their competition charges, so their rents are substantially below market. Such landlords congratulate themselves on always having tenants, but do not realize it is because they are offering such bargain rates. Other landlords know this but are terrified they will lose tenants if rents go up. Such landlords have no confidence in themselves or their properties.

I call this the *market rent flip* and will cover it in more detail in a later chapter. Here is a simplified version of how it works. Many landlords buy and sell rental properties based on some multiple of the monthly rent. This valuation method is called the *gross rent multiplier*. Such investors will say, "A rental house is worth 100 times the monthly rent." If the rent is $700 per month, then the house must be worth $70,000. If you buy a house for $70,000 that rents for $700 a month, and then simply raise the rent to market rates of $800 per month, you should be able to sell it for $80,000. There are more complicated evalua- tion methods discussed later, but the strategy is always the same.

People who engage in the market rent flip must be good at making phone calls and asking direct questions to discover what the market rents are in the area. They must have time to visit other rental properties to get a good sense of what people expect to have in a home at a certain rental rate. Market rent flippers must also be good networkers and natural salespeople who can find a tenant and rent the house fairly quickly. You do not have to have a career in sales—chairpersons who head committees must sell all the time in order to obtain volunteers; ministers must sell in order to grow their congregations rather than have people go to other churches; and teachers must sell the importance of what they are teaching in order to motivate children to learn. Think about the things you do, and whether they involve selling at all. If they do, and you are good at what you do, then you should be able to successfully handle a market rent flip.

Is it easy to flip vacant rental houses?

"Easy" is perhaps not the right word—every type of flip requires some amount of work. Think about this, though. When a home-owner wants to sell his or her home, he or she usually lists it with a real estate agent, who then places the property on the local MLS (Multiple Listing Service). All the other agents in town learn about that property and know they can make a commission if they bring a buyer. Even *for-sale-by-owner* (FSBO) houses have a wide variety of marketing vehicles to get the word out.

Usually, a vacant rental house has a lonely "For Rent" sign in the window or stuck into the front lawn, often faded by the sun after months without a tenant. Many times, after months of waiting, the owner will be thrilled to sell the house even at a price that is below the market, if only someone would make him or her an offer. This is the *vacancy flip*. You can buy the house and sometimes even obtain 100% seller financing. After all, the seller really wants regular income from the property and not necessarily a lump sum of money. It may not be necessary to lift a finger or spend a penny to improve the property. Simply find a tenant, put that tenant in place at market rents, and then sell the property to an investor.

The same type of person who would be ideal for a market rent flip would also be good at a vacancy flip, with one further requirement. For a vacancy flip, you will need to contact many landlords to see if they would be willing to sell their property. This is called *cold calling*. It involves a lot of rejection, as landlord after landlord tells you that he or she is not interested. If you can endure that rejection and stick to your plan, you will eventually find a landlord who does want to sell. Many people hate cold calling because they feel awkward making the first contact, and then they feel rejected afterward. If this is not a problem for you, you would be good at the vacancy flip.

How can I flip with no cash, no credit, and no power tools?

You can choose a strategy that involves virtually no risk at all, except your time. Most "no cash, no credit" plans involve finding a partner or finding a property owner willing to give you 100% financing. Faced with a direct question—"Will you let me buy your property for [X] thousand dollars with 100% financing, no money down, and a balloon payment in two years?"—most sellers will you turn you down without a second thought. Usually, the seller's mortgage says the whole loan will be due immediately if the owner sells the property, so he or she is not able to do 100% financing, even if he or she wanted to. That mortgage loan restriction is called a *due on sale clause*.

Here is a different question you can pose to someone who has already moved out of his or her home, or a landlord with a vacant rental house: "If I agree to sign a two-year lease at the rent you are asking, would you give me an option to buy the property at any time during the rental period for [X] thousand dollars?"

While these two questions may seem similar, the second one sounds more attractive, *and* it avoids the problem of the due on sale clause. This is the *tenant flip*.

Once you are in the house, you can clean it up, do some minor cosmetic improvements, and find a buyer who is willing to pay more than your agreed-upon option price. If you want to avoid two sets of closing costs—the one when you exercise your option to buy, and the one when you sell to the person you found—you need to make sure your lease says the option is assignable. Instead of actually buying the house, you simply sell your option to the buyer. The sales price for the option is the difference between what the buyer is willing to pay and what the option says you are allowed to pay.

I do not like fixing things up. Is there another kind of flip I can do?

You can tear down dilapidated pieces of property and flip the empty property. These are called *scrape flips* because you scrape the land clean and then sell it.

You would be surprised how often a vacant lot is worth more than the same land with a tumbled-down, old house on it. The house is usually too far gone to repair, so it scares off most buyers. Even bulldozing the home requires getting a permit, having access to some heavy equipment, and then taking the time to do it and haul off the debris. With the right contacts, though, you can subcontract that work for a relatively small sum, or partner with someone who has the equipment.

As with any flip, you will need to know what the going market rate is for similar vacant lots in your general geographic area. There is no point in buying a house and lot for $50,000, spending $5,000 to scrape it, and then having a vacant lot worth $50,000–$60,000. Also, be sure to research local attitudes about knocking down old houses just to build big new ones. Many neighborhoods resent this trend because it destroys the integrity and charm of the area. Local homeowners can become extremely vocal in their opposition, and may even successfully lobby the local government to impose new construction requirements that will make your land unsellable at a profit.

How does the option flip work?

Options are the rights to buy property, but without any obligation to actually go through with the purchase. When you have a lease with an option to buy, you are a tenant but you can choose to buy the property during an agreed time period for a predetermined price. Tenants are not the only people who can have options, though. If the property owner is willing, anyone can pay some money for a contract that gives him or her the right to buy the property at a set price in the future.

For example, say you pay Ollie Owner $1,000 for an option on his house. The option says you have the right to buy the house any time in the next six months for $89,000. It also says your option can be *assigned* (sold) to anyone else. The person who holds the option can then *exercise the option* and buy the home for $89,000 anytime within the six-month period.

You know that Brenda Buyer is willing to pay $99,000 for Ollie's house in exactly the same condition it is in now. You can take your option and sell it to Brenda for $10,000. Brenda pays you $10,000, and then pays Ollie $89,000. Brenda pays exactly the $99,000 she is willing to pay for the home. Ollie receives exactly the amount he wanted for his home. You make a total profit of $9,000 (the $10,000 option sale price minus the $1,000 you paid Ollie to secure the option), and you have no closing costs or holding costs and your name never appears in the real estate records.

With an option, though, you have to remember that the $1,000 you paid Ollie is not earnest money. It is the fully earned price for the option contract. Even if you do not find a buyer, Ollie gets to keep the $1,000.

Option flips can be very successful for people able to make cold calls and ask owners if they would be willing to option their properties. You also have to be good at networking in order to find buyers, because running ads in the paper may not be allowed unless you are the owner. Finally, you have to be able to afford the loss of the option price. In the previous example, if you are unable to find a buyer in six months, you will lose $1,000. You have to decide whether or not you can afford to lose this money. If you cannot afford to lose the $1,000 (or whatever the agreed-upon price is for the option), then you should not trade in options.

Again, there will be more specifics on options in Chapter 4.

I read about people getting rich flipping condos. How does that work?

Flipping condos is one type of what I call the *reservation flip*. The name comes from condo flipping, but it can apply to a wide variety of circumstances.

When a developer plans a condominium project, he or she must usually presell 50% or more of the units. This is done through a process called *reservations*, for which the purchaser pays an earnest money deposit. If the going rate for similar condos today is $149,000, the contract will entitle you to buy your condo when construction is finished for $149,000.

Let us say you put down earnest money in the amount of $5,000. The hope is that, eighteen months from now when the project is completed, similar condos are selling for $249,000. You have a contract that entitles you to buy a condo for $149,000. You can sell your contract to someone else for $80,000. That repays your earnest money and makes you a $75,000 profit. The buyer will be out the $80,000 he or she paid you, plus the $144,000 he or she will need to close, after crediting the earnest money. The buyer spends $224,000 total and receives a condo worth $249,000. Everyone wins as long as the market keeps going up dramatically.

That is the catch—that the music will stop before you have your seat. If the market is stagnant or declines, you will have to go through with the closing and will be stuck with a condo you cannot resell. Worse, you might be unable to borrow enough money to close and the developer will sue you. Many people have been driven into bankruptcy because of condo flips.

The reservation flip is not limited to condos. It can be done on any property for which you sign a firm purchase contract and then hope you will be able to sell the contract to someone else for a profit before you have to close. Remember, this is different from an option flip. With an option, you are under no obligation to complete the purchase. On the other hand, the money you pay for an option contract is not refundable.

Can I buy foreclosures as a type of flip?

Most people who buy foreclosure properties do so with plans to flip them. I have two books about buying foreclosure properties, *How to Make Money on Foreclosures* and *The Make Money on*

Foreclosures Answer Book. Read those books for more in-depth coverage. Generically, *foreclosure flips* include any type of forced sale during a time of economic distress—divorce, unpaid income or real estate taxes, judgment creditor seizures, lender foreclosures, or bankruptcy.

You can successfully buy foreclosure properties at below-market prices in three general circumstances.

1. The owner has 20% equity in the home but is willing to lose that equity and sell for the mortgage payoff balance, just to avoid the bad credit history and the trauma of a foreclosure.

2. The lender is about to foreclose and is willing to release its mortgage lien for less than the full payoff. Usually this works only when there is a local lender who owns the mortgage. If the mortgage has been sold on the national market, those new holders generally do not have the contractual or legal ability to work out a deal with you, even if they wanted to.

3. The lender has already foreclosed and the property has been on the market for 90 to 180 days without an acceptable bid. The time limit depends on the foreclosing owner's internal or government-imposed regulations. But, after some time, he or she will be allowed to accept almost any bid on the property, just to get it off the books. Remember, lenders are not in the business of making profits on selling real estate. They will even sell at a loss because their business model anticipates they will take losses on a certain number of loans and they price their interest rates accordingly.

To be successful at pre-foreclosure flips, you have to be very good at researching real estate titles to make sure you do not buy something that still has other liens or mortgages on it. Sure, you can and should buy title insurance when you are ready to buy. On the other hand, you do not want the expense of a third-party title search for every single property you are considering. You will have to learn how to do some of the work yourself. No special skills, other than knowing your market and being able to negotiate, are required for a post-foreclosure flip.

Is it possible to just find bargains, do nothing, and flip for a profit?

Of course it is possible, but there are not a lot of those deals floating around. The *under-market flip* depends on an unsophisticated seller who has no real estate agent or a poorly informed agent. The seller must have no idea regarding the true market value of the property, and you must get to him or her before all the other 8,000 bargain hunters looking for the same type of deal as you.

That being said, sometimes you just stumble upon those opportunities. I recently worked with a client who wanted some raw land on which to build a small retail development. I found a house and three acres of land in an area of rapid growth. As far as normal house values go, the seller's agent recommended a pretty high price of $653,000 for a modest 40-year-old ranch home with three bedrooms, one bathroom, and three acres of land. In any other part of town, that would be a $160,000 property, tops. With 43,560 square feet in an acre, and three acres of land (counting the house as worthless), the asking price worked out to $5 a square foot for the land. The seller's agent thought she was asking for the moon, but could get the price in such a hot market.

What I knew was that land was selling for $10 a square foot, only 1,000 feet down the road! If I were not working with a buyer client who needed just exactly that size property in that location, I could have bought it myself and flipped it. Even if I offered full price and agreed to pay all closing costs, I could have bought that property for around $660,000 and sold it the same day for $1.3 million! A house mover was willing to take the house away, at no expense to my client. I did not feel guilty about my client buying the property so cheaply because the seller and her agent set the price themselves. If they were happy with that sum, it was not my job to educate them that they could have gotten more.

Under-market flippers need to be very in tune with their market place and the range of prices for properties. They have to be good at networking to learn about new properties just coming on the market or about to be offered for sale. That is because the under-market flipper needs to be the first one to make an offer on the property, before everyone else learns about the bargain basement price. Finally, this type of flipper has to be good at making quick decisions. In this market, he or she who hesitates will lose the deal to someone faster.

What is the parcel flip?

It is a truism that, within certain limits, large pieces of property sell for less per-acre or per-square-foot than small pieces of property. In a semi-rural area, you might be able to buy ten acres of land for $10,000 an acre, or a total of $100,000. One-acre parcels large enough for a modest home or a mobile home might be selling for $20,000 an acre. If you were willing to make a smaller profit and charge less than current market prices, you could buy the property for $100,000 and sell ten parcels pretty quickly for a bargain price of $15,000 per acre. You have just made $50,000 simply by splitting a large piece of land into affordable, smaller pieces.

You might have to hire a surveyor to divide the property, or you might simply mark the boundaries on the land and have the buyer obtain his or her own survey. Usually, the buyer's lender will require a separate survey anyway. Be aware that many jurisdictions require permitting and local government approval before you can subdivide land into smaller parcels. Make sure this will not be a problem. Also, you want to make sure that property owners can obtain all the standard utilities fairly easily and that all health department requirements can be met if septic tanks will be necessary.

Parcel flipping requires no special skills except the ability to predict market demand. It is one thing to buy a house and be confident you can sell that one house for a profit. It is entirely different to know enough about your market to be sure that you can sell five or ten properties fairly quickly for a profit.

Condo conversions are specialized types of parcel flips. You buy a quadraplex or small apartment building, convert the units to condos, and then sell the condos individually. You will need the same skills as converting large land tracts into smaller ones, plus you will have some legal expenses associated with setting up the condominium documents.

Can I make money finding flipping opportunities for other people?

I have one big warning before answering this question. In many states, it is illegal for you to receive a fee or other compensation for helping someone find real estate opportunities, unless you have a real estate license. In California, for example, only licensed real estate professionals can find opportunities for flippers and receive a fee in return. To find out about your own state, check out Appendix E with the list of all state real estate licensing commissions and bureaus. Call, or visit their websites, and ask about any restrictions for your state.

In my own state of Alabama, for example, it is a Class A misdemeanor to receive compensation in exchange for scouting properties for someone else. It is punishable by up to one year in prison, and up to a $6,000 fine.

If allowed, you can be a *scout* for investors or flippers. As you can probably already tell, a flipper has to sift through a lot of information to find the right property that will translate into big profits. In order to work efficiently, a flipper will often pay scouts a small fee for tips regarding opportunities. The fee is usually $500 to $1,000, and the fee is paid only if the flipper buys the property he or she learned about from the scout. While the fee is not a lot on any one deal, if you are really hooked into your community, you could easily earn six, twelve, or even twenty scout fees a year. If an extra $3,000 to $20,000 a year would make a significant difference in your lifestyle, then you might want to think about this route.

To be successful, the scout needs to know almost as much as the flipper about the particular type of deals that interest the flipper. If you are just giving random, possibly useless information to your flipper, then you are the equivalent of a junk mailer, rather than a valuable resource. You will be ignored fairly quickly as you lose credibility.

Many scouts build up nest eggs from the fees and valuable experience gained from watching and listening to their flippers. Once their investments in these two areas reach critical mass, they are ready to go out and do their own flips.

What are the risks associated with flipping?

There are two major risks associated with flipping, but both are manageable. They are: (1) too little knowledge; and, (2) too much greed.

You gain knowledge through reading books, talking to mentors, and observing the behavior of successful people. You also need knowledge about yourself, though. Realistically, what are your strengths and weaknesses in terms of personality, time, money, access to credit, sophistication, salesmanship, and energy? What are your goals? Are they achievable with a conservative plan, or must you take huge risks in order to meet your self-imposed deadlines? Are you risk intolerant? If you do not like taking risks, you will never find a television flip that feels comfortable. Do not waste your time with that strategy. Instead, try another type of flip that suits you better.

Greed is an ugly thing because it does not seem like greed at the time. Instead, it feels like self-confidence that you have the "oomph" to pull off something incredible. My advice for beginning flippers: If you think your potential project will be dramatic and impress all your friends with your immense profits, think two or three more times before jumping at it.

To prevent greed from sneaking up on you, set realistic limits in advance and do not stray from them by more than an inch. In other words, if your requirement is to buy a property at 20% less than market value, do not buy one that is priced at 19% less than market value. You will want to, of course. You will say to yourself, "It's a great house. I can probably sell it for a little bit above market value and still make my same profit." It is a little bit like going to an auction. If you say in advance you will not pay over $250 for a leather sofa, you will not get sucked into a bidding war and find yourself paying $1,000 for an $800 piece of furniture.

There are plenty of deals out there. Wait for the right one for you.

Finally, always have a Plan B. Your Plan A is the one where you make a lot of money because all the stars are aligned and things work out perfectly. What if nothing works out well? What if everything goes wrong? Can you still sell the property and at least break even? Can you rent it to a tenant for enough money to cover your mortgage payments, insurance, and taxes, and then sell it later? There are several questions, later, devoted to managing surprises. Be sure to read them several times before starting your own flipping career.

How do I get started in flipping?
Here is a road map for beginning to flip houses.

1. Read several books on the subject by different authors. You need to get more than one perspective.

2. Evaluate your strengths and weaknesses, assets, and liabilities.

3. Establish reasonable goals that do not depend on good luck. One reader who writes to me regularly is 60 years old and wants to accumulate $4 million in five years, with little cash, no credit, and a full-time job he needs in order to pay his regular monthly bills. It is not going to happen! He will either get hurt badly jumping at the big deal he cannot afford, or he will do nothing at all for five years while he dreams about the big deal, just around the corner.

4. Pick *one* strategy that you think fits you and your goals. If

that requires additional education, such as taking classes in do-it-yourself home improvement, then make that investment.

5. Target a particular market area, such as one school district or a distinct submarket in your community. In Birmingham, Alabama, for example, submarkets might be the older Mountain Brook high-end homes, the new downtown loft market, or the Trussville-area expanding suburbia market. Learn everything you can about property values, rental rates, and demand growth in your target market. If necessary to your strategy, also learn construction and renovation permitting requirements, zoning, and other such issues.

6. Educate yourself about modern home improvement trends and pricing. The most efficient way to do this is to buy a weekend pass to the next home and garden show near you. Learn about remodeling, decorative finishes, landscaping, technology, and financing, all in one place. See a great range of prices and qualities, and compare products for yourself. Collect brochures, write down prices, and ask for samples. Talk to the experts, and ask pointed questions about details of installation, specialized tools, time required, and recommended subcontractors in your area. If you are willing to travel, it is a good idea to also visit the shows in nearby large cities.

7. Make a business plan. There are plenty of books and software on the market you can buy for under twenty dollars that will help you do this. Be sure to use conservative estimates regarding the amount of time and money you can

devote to your flipping business. All business plans have deadlines. You cannot say, "I will buy six housekeeper flips when I am able and sell them as soon as possible." You have to say, "I will buy and sell one housekeeper flip every three months." I have a sample business plan in Appendix B.

8. Follow your plan. Revisit your plan once a year to make adjustments learned through experience. Resist the urge to change your plan every time you have an "Ah-ha!" experience. Some thoughts need time for reflection, to mature.

Chapter 2

FINANCIALS

- How much money can I make flipping houses?
- Is it worth flipping houses if my profits will be small?
- Where do I get the cash I need to start flipping?
- What if I have no cash and bad credit—can I still flip?
- Where do I find the financing for a flip?
- What do I need to be careful about when borrowing money for a flip?
- Can I get 100% financing for a house flip?
- What is the truth about the no-money-down flipping strategies I see advertised?
- Should I have investors or partners?
- What should I know about the homeowner partnership strategy?
- How do I prepare a budget?
- How much will repairs cost?
- Who can help me with estimating repair expenses?
- Is there any way to avoid construction surprises?
- What tax issues do I need to know about?
- Can I shelter income with depreciation deductions?
- Will writing off my repair expenses help on my taxes?
- If I keep using my profits to buy more houses to flip, can I defer taxes under the tax-free exchange rules?
- Should I wait a year before reselling in order to take advantage of cheaper long-term capital gains rates?
- Are there any tax pitfalls to flipping?
- If I choose the homeowner flip, can I escape paying income taxes?
- What are some other tax issues I should know about?

How much money can I make flipping houses?

There is no limit to how much an experienced house flipper can make. I suggest for newbies that you limit yourselves to something you can buy for 10%–20% less than your break-even price. If you think you can sell a house for $160,000, after fixing it up and holding it for six months, then you have to work backward to find your maximum purchase price.

Example (I invented these numbers. Do not use them as a guide for your project.):

1. Three-bedroom, two-bath brick homes in this neighborhood typically sell for $160,000 after three months on the market.

2. The house I want to buy will require $15,000 worth of work and be ready for resale two months after I buy it—three months if I run into delays.

3. As a result, I can anticipate having interest expenses, insurance, taxes, and utility payments for six months. These will probably total another $7,200. (I usually estimate interest on the high side. Six months of interest on $128,000 at 8% annual interest is $5,120. Then it is just a matter of estimating utilities and other expenses.)

4. My share of the purchase and selling closing costs will be around $2,000.

5. Math:

Sales price	$160,000
Minus Repair Expenses	−15,000
Minus Holding Expenses	−7,200
Minus Closing Expenses	−2,000
Equals	$135,800

If you bought this house for $135,800 and sold it for $160,000, you would break even, assuming you did not have to pay a real estate commission or any marketing expenses.

You want to buy this house for 10%–20% less than your break-even price. Ten percent of $135,800 is $13,580. Twenty percent of $135,800 is $27,160. You can afford to buy this house for $108,640 ($135,800 − $27,160) to $122,220 ($135,800 − $13,580), depending on your particular margin requirements. Your profit would be $13,580 to $27,160.

Is it worth flipping houses if my profits will be small?

This is one of those questions each person must answer for him- or herself. If your first flip gives you a profit of $2,000, but you spent 320 hours—eight solid weeks of eight-hour days—of your own time on the project, that works out to $6.25 per hour. Was it worth it? Might you have been better off taking a part-time job flipping burgers instead of houses? Perhaps. But, you have to ask yourself how much the education was worth. If the experience prepared you to do another flip, make three times as much money, and spend one-third as much time, you will make a little over $56 per hour on your next flip. Now is it worth it?

You have to define your goals for the flipping venture. Do you want to pick up some extra cash for a slush fund, vacation plans, or simply to pay down your credit card? If your goals are modest, your profits can be modest, also. If your goals are much larger, start out with fairly easy, fast flips such as option flips or housekeeping flips. Or, do a homeowner flip that gives you at least two years to make all your renovations, and then sell at a profit with absolutely no income taxes if your profit is under the current $250,000 ($500,000 for married couples) limit.

Where do I get the cash I need to start flipping?

The best place to find cash is in a deal that does not require any upfront money. This would include being a scout, leasing a house with an option to purchase it in the future, buying a home for your personal residence, or buying a fixer-upper property significantly below eventual market value.

Scouts earn fees from flippers by finding deals for them. You can save your fees until you have enough for a down payment for your own flip.

Renting a house with a purchase option usually requires only the first month's rent and a security deposit. Better yet, you might want to help a friend or relative find a rental house with a purchase option. Your friend pays the rent and security deposit, your friend lives there, but he or she assigns the option to you. You have no money in the deal at all, but you can still sell your option to someone else at a profit. In other words, if the option gives you the right to buy the house for $129,000, but the house is really worth $139,000, someone might buy your option for $5,000. That gives him or her the right to buy the house for $139,000, making a total outlay for him or her of $144,000. The house is really worth $149,000, so they get a bargain. The landlord gets the amount of money he wanted, and you make $5,000 on the transaction with no money down.

Homeowners can often borrow 100% of the money necessary to

buy their personal residence. If you do this and use the homeowner flip strategy you can get started with no cash.

Commercial lenders will loan you 100% of the purchase price of a property, plus the money necessary for repairs and holding expenses, if the final value of the house after repairs will be at least 25% to 31% more than the loan. I once borrowed $200,000 for a house flip—$150,000 for the entire purchase price plus an extra $50,000 for repairs and holding costs. When the repairs were finished, the house was worth $350,000.

As flipping becomes more popular, though, the no-cash deals will not be as plentiful as they once were. If you need some cash for a down payment and for expenses, and it is not sitting in your bank account, where do you find it? Investors are one solution. Plenty of doctors, lawyers, high-commission salespeople, professional gamblers, and other such people are always looking for real estate investments. Some books recommend going to friends and family, but I discourage this. An investor understands that he or she is putting money at risk, and that he or she might lose the investment. Friends and family do not usually understand that, no matter how hard you try to explain it to them. They trust you and think failure is impossible. If the unthinkable happens, and you lose their money, you might damage that relationship forever.

Under the right circumstances, you can borrow money from your retirement account to make investments. Check with your plan administrator for the rules and details.

A home equity line of credit might be the answer. You borrow whatever you need for the down payment and expenses of a flip, and then repay the home equity loan when the flip sells. Similar, but more expensive, is using your credit card to fund the flip. I do not recommend this for most people, but sometimes it is the only way you will be able to get the money. If it is the only way to get the money, though, think about whether or not the risk and high interest rates are worth it to you.

You also might want to think about what you are willing to sell to finance your flip. Are you willing and able to give up a second car in order to save the money for a real estate investment? What about vacations, a boat, new audio equipment, season football tickets, or 832 cable television channels? Save your way to a down payment by examining what is important in your life and what you can trim out of the budget.

What if I have no cash and bad credit—can I still flip?

With no cash and no credit, you will need a partner or investor to take advantage of the whole array of different kinds of flips. That is not always possible, though. Instead, you might want to choose a type of flipping strategy that does not require cash or credit.

You can start as a scout for someone else, gaining valuable experience and using your fees to build up a nest egg for your own flips. At the same time, clean up any credit problems you might have.

In the alternative, you can do the tenant flip, which involves finding a rental house and a landlord willing to give you an option to buy the property. You can live in the house yourself, or talk a friend or acquaintance into subleasing it from you. Just make sure the tenant assigns the purchase option to you. Read Chapter 4 for more details.

Sometimes property owners will give you 100% financing for a short period of time, perhaps a year or so. Especially if you are going to be making modest improvements that do not involve any demolition, they might be very motivated to let you have a shot at flipping the house. Worst probable case for them—you clean the property, repaint, improve the landscaping, make minor cosmetic repairs, and then default and cannot pay off the loan because you cannot flip the house. The owner forecloses and ends up with a house in better shape than when she sold it to you, plus the mortgage payments during the time of your ownership. Worst nightmare for them—you tear out five walls, all the cabinets, plumbing fixtures and carpet, and then default. If you know this fear in advance, though, you can take steps to assure the seller it will not happen.

Where do I find the financing for a flip?

While mortgage companies are an important source of funds for home buyers, most flippers need to look for commercial loan money. That used to mean regular banks only. Today, though, credit unions also loan money for short-term investments. Their interest rates will usually be at least 1% higher than home loan interest rates.

Be sure to shop carefully for your loan. Some lenders quote interest rates as "prime plus 1%," while others might quote you "150 basis points over *LIBOR*." One hundred fifty basis points is the same as 1.5%, so that translates to LIBOR (or London Interbank Offered Rate, which is an interest rate index for loans that banks make to each other) plus 1.5%. The trick is, LIBOR is often much lower than prime, so "prime plus 1" might be a higher interest rate than "LIBOR plus 1.5."

You might be able to obtain seller financing for many flips. Especially with rental houses, the owner is usually comfortable receiving a monthly check from his or her property. That check can be rent, or it can be your mortgage payment—it usually does not matter. Be careful of one thing, though. Many owners who hold financing do so for income tax reasons. They do not want a lot of income in any one year, which they would have with a straightforward sale. Those owners might have a prepayment penalty in the loan documents you sign. The prepayment penalty might require you to pay extra money, usually as much as 10%, if you pay off the loan before the maturity date. A penalty like that can dramatically change the economics of your flip, so be careful.

What do I need to be careful about when borrowing money for a flip?

If you are doing any type of renovation or remodeling work, make sure you borrow money for a long enough period of time. Always estimate on the high end for your expenses, and be sure to add into your loan request the money you will need for interest expenses, taxes, insurance, and utilities during the remodeling period. You do not have to hide them somewhere by, for example, doubling your estimate for painting expenses. Commercial lenders expect to see those holding costs included in your loan request. Appendix A has a sample loan request to use as a guide. In addition, avoid being too optimistic about how long it will take to complete your work and sell the house. Give yourself some leeway. Lenders like conservative, careful borrowers.

Several things about a commercial loan are different from the home loan of your experiences. The most significant ones are explained as follows.

Commercial loans usually require more paperwork and expenses. You might be required to produce a survey showing boundary lines and all improvements, an *Environmental Questionnaire*, a *Phase I Environmental Report*, architectural drawings, and proof of builder's risk and liability insurance, not just property insurance. The lender might require you to hire a third-party general contractor rather than supervising the work yourself. The title insurance requirements might include many things that will make the policy more expensive. Some out-of-state commercial lenders use out-of-state law firms for the closing documents, which could lead to attorney's fees dramatically higher than those you might have had in previous experiences.

Always ask each potential lender for a copy of its checklist for the closing attorney, the names of the attorneys it generally uses, and an estimate of the total fees. This will tell you who uses local talent, who uses inexpensive attorneys, and who has a long list of requirements that might cost you time, trouble, and money.

Make sure you understand the interest rate and how often the rate will change. Home loan rates might change once or twice a year. Commercial loan rates will change rates every time the index—the reference point—changes.

Find out what fees you will be expected to pay. This could include an origination fee equal to 0.5%–1% of the loan, plus disbursement or inspection fees. In other words, the lender might require an independent third party to provide regular progress reports of your remodeling or repairs. The fee can be several hundred dollars per inspection. You might have to pay a fee every time the lender advances money to you to pay bills. Knowing that, you might want to draw down loan money once a month instead of four times a week, every time a bill comes in the mail.

Ask about the draw schedule if you are borrowing money for renovations or repairs. One lender might limit you to once-a-month checks. Another could have a specific schedule, such as "30% of the loan will be disbursed when all the rough carpentry, electrical, and plumbing has been completed, and not before." Some require you to pay part of every bill presented to the lender. If the month's construction bills total $4,000, the lender might disburse $3,200 (80%) and you must come up with the other $800 from your personal funds.

Do not let any of this scare you. I do not know of a single lender who does every one of these things, and some do not do any of them. You just have to shop wisely instead of being surprised after you sign on the dotted line.

Can I get 100% financing for a house flip?

If you have a good relationship with a local banker, excellent credit, and other significant assets besides your home and retirement account, you can usually obtain 100% financing for a flip. Unfortunately, most people do not qualify for such favorable terms.

There is a funny loophole that we can use, however. Most people who buy real estate will be able to borrow 75% or 80% of the appraised value or the purchase price, whichever is *less*. This prevents you from being able to borrow the entire purchase price just because you were brilliant and found an incredible bargain. On the other hand, if you have a credible plan to improve the property, you can base your borrowing on what the house will be worth when you are finished, not today's purchase price or appraised value.

Loan to Value Calculation

Suppose you need to borrow $160,000 to buy and fix up a house, and you want to obtain 100% financing from a lender who requires the loan to be 75% of the completed value of the house. How much does the house need to be worth to support this loan?

$$\frac{75}{100} \text{ is the same as } \frac{\$160,000}{\text{what number?}}$$

160,000 x 100 = 16,000,000
16,000,000 ÷ 75 = $213,333

Most people would intuitively say the house must be worth $200,000, or 25% more than the loan. But, if the house is worth $200,000 and you borrow $160,000, your loan-to-value ratio is too high—it will be 80%. In reality, you must increase the value by 33.3% for the loan to be 75% of the final value.

Other than this loophole, or excellent connections with a banker, you will generally be able to secure 100% financing in only two circumstances. The first is if you do a homeowner flip of your own residence. In many circumstances, you can still get 100% of the money to buy a personal residence. The other circumstance is the lease option flip, in which you are not really borrowing money at all. In reality, you are just renting a house with the right to buy it (and resell it the same day) if you exercise your option. Remember, though, not all leases have options in them. This is a separately negotiated item with the landlord.

What is the truth about the no-money-down flipping strategies I see advertised?

The truth is that almost anyone can buy and sell properties with no money down. The other truth is that the strategies are usually low-profit and can be high-risk if you do not spend the massive amounts of time necessary to avoid all possible problems. If you have no other options, you can go for it, but be careful. Avoid spending what little money you have on seminars and DVDs on the subject. The primary thrust of these marketing pitches is to get you excited so you will spend more money to buy the promoters' products. If no-money-down deals were so easy to do and so easy to find, would promoters be selling seminars to you?

Should I have investors or partners?

If you need the experience, wisdom, or skills of another person, then take him or her on as a partner. If you need money, access to credit, or contacts, take someone on as an investor but not as a partner. Sometimes you do not have a choice. The people with the money often want to be partners, so they can be close to the action and help make decisions to protect their money.

Here are the pros and cons of investors and partners. You decide what you need based on your circumstances.

Table: Pros and Cons of Investors vs. Partners

	Investors	Partners
Pros:	• Usually bring money • Do not meddle in decisions • Feelings will not be hurt if you do not include them in the next deal • Understand it is just business, and there is some risk involved	• Usually bring skills, and sometimes money • Help you make the right decisions • Can help with time-consuming tasks and chores
Cons:	• Do not provide any assistance with advice, time, work, or materials • May require you to cut your losses and sell early if things take too long • Often require a predetermined dollar return, not just a percentage of the profits	• Most decisions require discussions and consensus • Personal problems may interfere with their assistance on the project • Because partners are usually friends before they are partners, a financial loss may destroy a friendship • Feelings might be hurt if you do not include them in the next deal

If you do join forces with investors or partners, make sure you put everything in writing. Your relationship should be clearly defined, along with everybody's expectations, contributions, and decision-making authority. Make sure you describe what will happen if there are problems or the project turns into a financial disaster. Can the investor demand his or her money early or take over the project completely? Can your partner refuse to perform any more work but still demand a percentage of the profits? These and other similar questions should be worked through with the assistance of a lawyer or a business consultant.

Choose the right structure if you are going to have partners. Details are beyond the scope of this book, but there are generally three common ways to set up a partnership. The most common is what is called a *general partnership*. Any partner can make decisions that bind the entire partnership. You are all equally liable for 100% of the partnership debts—not just your share of the debts. At the simplest level, there are no formalities and no paperwork. Next up in complexity is a *limited liability company*. It requires formal paperwork, usually prepared by a lawyer. A lengthy document sets out all the procedures for operating the company. Members are protected from liability unless they sign guarantee agreements for loans or other liabilities. Finally, a *subchapter S corporation* is very similar to a limited liability company, but generally provides more flexibility regarding long-range plans.

What should I know about the homeowner partnership strategy?

Many homeowners know their houses can be sold for a handsome profit, if only they had the time, skills, or money to fix them up. Unfortunately, they lack some or all of the ingredients. Some flipping experts recommend that you partner with homeowners. The homeowner supplies the property and sometimes even the cash for improvements. You provide the know-how and the labor. At the end of the process, you market and sell the house and split the profits in a pre-agreed proportion.

I do not recommend this strategy because it has so many opportunities for misunderstandings or abuse. The biggest risk is that the homeowner will be uncooperative during the renovation or repair process and effectively sabotage your efforts. At the end, he or she could have a much more valuable home, and you could have nothing. Be careful!

If you insist on using this strategy, though, you must have two things to be successful. One is an option agreement allowing you to buy the property at its current fair market value at an amount set out in the option. The other thing you need is a very clearly written contract, in plain English, listing each party's responsibilities and expectations. Include a budget and a timeline. Who will be responsible for lawn care and keeping the house clean during the marketing period? If some home furnishings and clutter will need to be in storage during the marketing period, put that in writing, along with who will pay for the storage.

Be sure to specify how the profits will be split and if the profits will be calculated before or after rehab, holding, and sale expenses. Include several examples of calculations, including a best-case, most-likely-case, and worst-case scenario. Discuss and write down your agreements regarding what will happen if things go wrong. What if the homeowner does not keep the house clean during the marketing period and intentionally or accidentally sabotages your efforts, and as a result, the house does not sell? Are you just out of luck, can you force the owner to pay for the value of your services and expenses, or can you take a lien on the property? You may need the assistance of an attorney for some of these issues.

Most states will allow an option holder to market property as if it were his or her own. If you try to sell someone else's property, but do not have some type of ownership interest or option, you could be guilty of selling real estate without a license. Check with your state's real estate commission before embarking on this strategy. Ask specifically about your ability to market and sell property in which you have an option interest only. A list of real estate licensing authorities and their websites is in Appendix E.

How do I prepare a budget?

Three items are essential for a budget: (1) a checklist of things to include in the budget; (2) accurate figures for those items; and, (3) a timeline of how long everything will take.

Overlooking the little things can add up to big money. Most first-time flippers do not think about debris removal, permit fees, builder's risk insurance, liability insurance, inspection fees, subcontractor license fees, utilities, and small tools. They are often overly optimistic regarding the time everything will take. Many completely fail to take into account normal delays caused by work stoppage until the local government inspection can be completed for that stage.

Subcontractor license fees

In most localities you must obtain a building permit before you can begin remodeling or renovating a property. When the project is completed, you must submit a list of the names and addresses of your subcontractors, ask for a final inspection, and request a *Certificate of Occupancy* (C/O). The C/O allows someone to move in— no buyer is going to pay top dollar for a property without a C/O. If some of your subcontractors do not have business licenses, you will not be able to obtain your C/O until you pay for their business licenses or at least the license fees that would have been attributable to your job. To avoid nasty surprises, always make sure your subcontractors have current business licenses.

How much will repairs cost?

Repair and remodeling costs can vary widely depending on your part of the country, local competition among subcontractors, the quality of your finishes, and the existence and number of surprises. *Finishes* are things like carpet, wall coverings, door quality, and countertops, and can be a significant part of your costs. A paint-grade hollow core door is much cheaper than a solid oak door, for example.

Surprises can increase your repair costs, too. For example, a few years ago I was flipping an older home and had a firm quote of $1,500 to replace all the plumbing fixtures. However, we pulled off crumbling plaster, and revealed pipes that were brittle with age. The plumber also discovered that the entire sanitary sewer line to the street was crumbling and needed to be replaced, the plumbing repair bill went from $1,500 to $6,000.

As you can see, there are really two issues when it comes to estimating: (1) how to estimate your reasonable expenses; and, (2) how to cut down on the number of surprises.

Who can help me with estimating repair expenses?

Lowes, Home Depot, 84 Lumber, and other national or local home improvement stores usually have estimating services to assist you. Simply tell them the general nature of the work, such as replacing cabinets or installing a new bathroom. Next, pick out some item, such as a wall cabinet or a tub, that represents the quality of the whole project. After obtaining some measurements from you, the home improvement store can give you a fairly accurate estimate of your costs.

You can also go online and do this yourself. One of my favorite sites is **www.contractor.com**. The specific page for estimating is at **www.contractors.com/h/info/resources.html**. It might be a good idea to get estimates from your home improvement store and online, and see how close they are to each other. If there is a significant difference, ask someone at the store to explain the possible reasons.

Whenever possible, ask for firm bids from subcontractors. Subcontractors will give you a wide range of prices. This is usually because of the following reasons.

1. Some bid very low because of mistakes or misjudgment.

2. Some bid very low because their *scope of work* does not include many standard items for which you will have to execute expensive change orders after the work has started.

3. Some bid very low because their overhead is low—they have no offices, no liability insurance, no workers' compensation insurance, and perhaps other matters that should scare you away from them.

4. Some bid very high because they allow for too much cushion in case something goes wrong or their workers damage materials or perform work improperly and must redo it.

5. Some bid very high because they use a pricing model called *value pricing*, which is based on what the market will bear, not what it costs to complete the job, plus a fair profit.

6. Some will give you a reasonable price based on the anticipated time and materials, plus something extra to cover general business overhead expenses, plus a reasonable profit.

As you become more experienced, you will have a better feel for what the bids should be. While you are still a beginner, though, my advice is to get as many bids as possible, read the fine print about what is not covered in the bid, and ask questions if you do not understand something. There is nothing wrong with saying, "Your bid is twice as much as Acme's bid. I'm not trying to beat you down on your price, I just want to understand the difference, and why I should choose you. Can you help me with that?"

Is there any way to avoid construction surprises?

While you can manage your risk by choosing projects with a very low likelihood of surprises, you cannot guarantee that you will avoid construction surprises entirely. Beautiful Victorian homes are like horror movies for flippers—something bloodthirsty is waiting behind every wall, ceiling, and floor. Instead of trying to flip a Victorian home, look for something boring, like a ten- to fifteen-year old one-story ranch house with brick siding. As you gain experience, you can become more adventurous. No doubt about it, the larger profits are in the projects that scare off other people. As a beginner, though, you should be one of the scared flippers instead of one of the fearless ones.

I strongly recommend you hire a reputable, independent home inspector before finalizing your purchase. Real estate agents and mortgage brokers like home inspectors who do not make waves and flunk properties. Take recommendations from those groups with a grain of salt. Repair people like tough home inspectors who find lots of repair work. Rely more heavily on recommendations from heating and air conditioning people, plumbers, and electricians.

The most likely source of expensive surprises is rotten wood in the attic, flooring, eaves, or around windows. After that, electrical wiring in very old homes is usually substandard and must be completely replaced, not just repaired. Those same homes might have only 60-amp or 100-amp service from the power company. For modern electricity loads, especially if you have electric heat or air conditioning, you will need 200-amp service. That will cost more money. Because most plumbing components are in the walls and between floors, they can lead to nasty surprises. Finally, new flippers should never try to repair old plaster. Rip it out, and replace it with drywall. Leave *restoration*—meaning a return to the original condition—to the experts.

What tax issues do I need to know about?

Forget everything you have ever heard about the tax advantages of investing in real estate. If you are a serious flipper, meaning you intend to do several flips a year, you will not be able to take most of the tax deductions and benefits. That is because you are not an investor—you are someone who buys at wholesale and sells at retail, just like Wal-Mart. On the other hand, if you do one flip every year or two, you can probably still take advantage of the normal tax breaks. Specific tax issues are addressed in the following questions.

Can I shelter income with depreciation deductions?

The essence of a *depreciation deduction* is the theory that real estate improvements will decrease in value if you hold them for a long period of time. You can write off part of that decrease every year. The essence of a flip is to get in and get out quickly. The two theories do not really belong in the same boat. You normally will have no opportunity to use any depreciation deductions, and might not even be allowed to do so, even if you have the opportunity under IRS rules. If you have any questions about your particular circumstances, you should discuss them with a tax professional who knows your property, your overall tax picture, and your particular goals.

Will writing off my repair expenses help on my taxes?

Writing off your repair expenses provides benefits only if you straddle a tax year with your flip. In other words, you buy the property in November of one year, make repairs for several months, and then sell the property in April of the next year. You will need to be very careful about characterizing something as a repair if the IRS thinks it is a *capital improvement*. Repairs can be written off on your taxes. Capital improvements are added to your purchase price and have the result of reducing your taxable profit on a resale.

If I keep using my profits to buy more houses to flip, can I defer taxes under the tax-free exchange rules?

It depends. If you flip one house every one or two years, you might be able to take advantage of something called a *tax-free exchange*. This tax break is limited to investors, though. If you flip too often, you might not be considered an investor. When it comes to aggressive tax accounting, you are much better off taking the advice of a paid professional than trying to do it yourself using self-help books.

Let us suppose, however, you do qualify for the tax-free exchange. Here is how it works. First, it is not really tax free. You do pay the taxes eventually, usually on the built-up profits after you sell your last property and do not buy another one. In a nutshell, the IRS says you do not have to pay income taxes in the current year on your profits if you sell one property, buy another one of equal or greater value, and invest all your cash from the first sale in the purchase of the second property. The new property is called the *replacement property*. You must identify the replacement property within 45 days of selling your old property. You must complete the purchase of the replacement property within 180 days or by the due date of your income tax return for the year of the sale, whichever comes first. There are also other requirements; to learn more, look for articles or websites that discuss *1031 exchanges* (pronounced ten-thirty-one), *Starker exchanges*, or *tax-deferred exchanges*.

Should I wait a year before reselling in order to take advantage of cheaper long-term capital gains rates?

Depending on the numbers, this might make sense for you. As with all other things, the IRS takes the position that long-term capital gains rates—currently at a maximum of 15% of your profits—are only for investors. Flippers are not usually investors. But, if you do one or two flips every year, you might qualify. As with all the other IRS rules that have no firm guidelines, it depends on the circumstances. Ask a tax professional for advice.

Sometimes, it does not make economic sense to drag out a sale, even if you do get cheaper tax rates. You should first determine how much you will save in taxes. Then, you should compare that number to how much your additional interest, real estate taxes, insurance, lawn care, and utilities will cost you if you hold the property and wait to sell it. Then, judge if it makes economic sense to delay a sale or not. Also ask yourself, if you have a buyer today, if you want to risk him or her disappearing later.

Are there any tax pitfalls to flipping?

Most people who buy and sell property pay the income taxes on their profits but do not think about self-employment taxes for Social Security and Medicare. If the IRS audits you and successfully argues that you are in the business of flipping properties, it might assess the self-employment taxes, plus penalties and interest. There are no clear-cut rules regarding when you are an investor and when you are in the business of flipping properties.

Obtain good tax advice from someone you trust, preferably a paid professional and not your cousin's friend who is in business school.

If I choose the homeowner flip, can I escape paying income taxes?

Under current tax law, you absolutely can escape paying income taxes on a certain amount of your profit. The homeowner flip is not a fast flip, like some of the others, but it is still a strategy to own or control property for a short period of time, improve its value, and sell at a profit. Tax laws in effect when this book was written allow homeowners to sell their principal residence and make up to $250,000 in profit ($500,000 for married persons) as long as they owned and lived in the property during two of the last five years. In other words, if you lived in the house for the first two years, and then rented the house out for the last three years, you can take advantage of this tax break. You can do this type of flip every two years with these same tax benefits for as long as the tax break exists.

What are some other tax issues I should know about?

There are many other tax issues besides income taxes. Most counties and parishes charge a *recordation tax* based on the dollar value of a sale. That can amount to many thousands of dollars of additional fees at closing. Some communities have what is called a *mansion tax*. It is a local government tax on residential real estate sales over a certain amount—whatever is considered a *mansion* under local law.

Especially when flipping raw land, you should know about something called *rollback taxes*. Raw land is not just vast tracts out in the middle of nowhere. You might buy a home on a double lot, flip the house on one lot and sell the second lot separately to someone else.

Or, you might buy a small three- or five-acre farmette in a growing suburban area and sell the extra land.

If property has a low real estate tax rate because its current use is agricultural or residential, for example, and then it is sold and converted to a convenience store, the real estate taxes will be higher. Normally, this would not be a problem for the seller, unless the sales contract had a clause requiring that taxes be prorated, including prior year taxes. When a jurisdiction has rollback tax rights, it can recalculate the real estate taxes going back as many as ten years. The seller might have to reimburse the buyer for ten years' worth of taxes at very high rates, possibly amounting to more than the sales price of the property.

For all these issues, and any others not mentioned, a title insurance company or real estate closing company can tell you what possible taxes you might have to consider. Any real estate agent can tell you the closing companies in town, and the closing companies can answer your questions for you.

Chapter 3

FINDING AND BUYING A HOUSE TO FLIP

- What is the ideal first flip?
- How do I find a house to flip before everyone else finds it?
- Who can give me the best leads on property that is for sale that would make a profitable flip?
- How can I encourage sellers to find me?
- Can I find properties simply by reading the home sale magazines?
- Is there a public version of the Multiple Listing Service that professionals use?
- What homes should I avoid?
- I do not have time for research. What are easy sources of flip opportunities?
- What happens at a foreclosure?
- Is it better to wait and buy after the foreclosure auction?
- How do I find post-foreclosure properties?
- How much should I offer?
- Should I obtain an appraisal for all properties before I buy?
- How do I estimate value?
- When I am comparing property sales, what features affect value?
- Is there a way to find out the actual sales prices for houses so I can evaluate the comparables?
- What are holding costs, and how much can I expect to pay?
- What is the best way to present my offer?
- Do I need a contract form, or can I use the one that real estate agents use?
- If the property is a fixer-upper, do I need a home inspection clause in the contract?
- What is the normal earnest money amount?
- I would like to specify seller financing in my offer. Does that require any special language?
- What can I do to make my offer more attractive to a seller?

- What happens if the seller accepts my offer?
- Can I cancel a contract if my due diligence reveals the flip will not work?
- Are there any technical requirements for canceling a contract?
- What can I expect at closing?

What is the ideal first flip?

The best first flip will give you a modest profit but, at the same time, eliminate most of the types of risks that can attack the inexperienced. I like to look at the risks in a question format and then separate them into categories, and then eliminate anything that fits into a bad category.

- **Risk Category 1**—If you obtain an education from books like this one, and do the work necessary, you can overcome the following risks.

  - What prices are similar houses selling for?
  - How long are similar houses on the market?
  - How much will known repairs cost?
  - How long will minor repairs take?
  - Will I meet any resistance from neighborhood architectural control committees, historic preservation societies, or similar groups?
  - What will my purchase, holding, and sale costs be?

- **Risk Category 2**—The risks on the next list are harder to control if you do not have experience.

  - How long will major repairs take?
  - How do I obtain the best price for repairs, without running the risk of shoddy, second-rate work?

- **Risk Category 3**—Finally, the following risks are the unforeseeable, surprise risks. If you have the financial staying power to overcome them, you will not get hurt. If you are a novice without substantial resources or the ability to borrow additional money, you could have a disaster.

  - If the project is a major one, will the market conditions change before my renovation is completed?
  - Will renovation uncover major defects that must be corrected at substantial additional expense?

Knowing these things, you want to find a piece of property that does not involve anything in the second two risk categories. Avoid major repairs, trying to chisel the last penny out of a subcontractor, lengthy projects, and homes that are very old, very dilapidated, or the recent objects of do-it-yourself major renovations. For example, my brother once bought a home with several new bedrooms, a bathroom, and a family room added by the prior owner. The *wall studs*—the 2x4s holding up the drywall and the ceiling—were placed 8 feet apart instead of the normal 16 inches. All the outlets and lights ran back to the same circuit breaker, which tripped constantly. The only way to fix that house was to start over.

I recommend ten- to twenty-year-old, single-story houses with brick veneer, built on a concrete slab. Look for three bedrooms and two bathrooms, so you do not have to add any extra rooms. This is a very marketable style and size of home. If you cannot sell it for some reason, you can always rent it out. Any structural problems, such as settling, have had a chance to reveal themselves. Major problems, such as a complete electrical or plumbing overhaul, or rotted wood at the windows, have usually not had time to develop. The house may need a new roof, but any reputable roofer can give you a firm quote after inspecting the rafters for rot.

Older houses may have environmental problems with asbestos insulation, asbestos tile floors, and lead-based paint. They are also more likely to have cloth-covered electrical wiring, or aluminum wiring, both of which are undesirable. An older home might have insufficient amperage service, requiring a complete electrical upgrade. Many older homes were covered in an insulating material that actually soaks up moisture like a sponge, resulting in mold, mildew, and odor problems.

How do I find a house to flip before everyone else finds it?

The first step in finding a house is to define the house you want. If you take the attitude that you do not know exactly what you want but you will recognize it when you see it, then you are headed for trouble. One of two things will happen. Either you will spend far too much time looking at everything and become discouraged, or you will jump on something inappropriate, simply because it has some emotional appeal, and end up getting hurt.

Pick a flipping strategy from Chapter 1. Are you looking for a housekeeper flip, television flip, vacancy flip, or something else? List the characteristics of a property fitting your strategy. Then ask yourself: "If I cannot see these characteristics from the street or find them from public sources, how do I find out about them?" Appendix D has a list of possible sources of information about potential flip opportunities. One example is cleaning services that specialize in fire damage or other insurable losses. Often, the homeowner has a large insurance check to pay for the repairs but is too traumatized by the event to tackle renovation. Many of them would be willing to sell the house to you for little money and assign the insurance check to you.

Next, I suggest targeting a particular neighborhood or two, or a particular school district. Learn everything you can about the area, including market rents for houses, sales prices for homes, major employers for residents, and the local churches, grocery stores, and community centers. Make a note of any houses with poorly maintained lawns, peeling paint, constant "for rent" signs, or indications they are vacant. Write down the addresses. Call the local tax assessor to find out the names and mailing addresses of the owners. You want to be the local expert for the area you picked.

Now you are ready. You find flip opportunities by looking for "for sale" signs on suitable properties or by cold calling potential sellers in the area you targeted. Remember, a lot of people you cold call will tell you they are not interested. You have to be able to handle rejection gracefully. On the plus side, though, today's rejection might be tomorrow's prospect or might refer other prospects to you. The trick is to stay in touch, even if you have been rejected.

Naturally, you do not want to keep asking the same people if they want to sell their houses to you. Instead, mail them note cards once or twice a month. Ask them for referrals, and offer to pay a referral fee if allowed under state law. (Contact your local real estate commission to find out whether or not it is legal to pay referral fees to someone who is not a licensed real estate agent. Contact information can be found in Appendix E.) If you are just asking for referrals, you will not feel like a pest. Of course, if that homeowner decides to sell, you will be the first person he or she calls.

Who can give me the best leads on property that is for sale that would make a profitable flip?

Think about all the people likely to come into frequent contact with troubled homeowners looking for a quick sale. Quickly, before you read my following suggestions, write down a description of all those people. If you wait until after you see my list, your mind will not be able to work as creatively.

These are the ones that spring to my mind.

- *Divorce lawyers.* They generally encounter high concentrations of people with money problems. They also usually do not practice bankruptcy law, so they would be glad to refer people to you for help.

- *Nursing home staff.* Many elderly family members are moved to nursing homes or other assisted living facilities by their loved ones. Most will never return to their homes again. Those homes usually have years of deferred minor repairs, accumulated dirt and grime, and a lifetime of sentimental but otherwise worthless objects cluttering the attic and house. The family needs a quick solution that involves minimal time and money. You can be the answer.

- *Ministers.* Like bankers and lawyers, they are not allowed to give you any names, but they do come to know about a lot of people in trouble. A minister is generally a nurturing person who wants to help, so he or she will be motivated to give your telephone number to other people, should they find themselves in need of your services.

- *Self-storage operators.* When people see a possible foreclosure looming, many of them start putting stuff in storage, just in case. They also tend to be remarkably candid with the manager of the self-storage facility about financial problems motivating them to seek storage. Cultivate relationships with the self-storage operators in your targeted part of town and you will find yourself with a steady stream of information regarding potential flips.

- *Title pawn, paycheck advance, and quick-cash businesses.* These businesses get to hear a lot of sad stories. Sometimes they simply cannot loan additional money to someone in trouble. They can hand someone your business card, though, or ask the applicant for permission to give his or her name to you.

How can I encourage sellers to find me?

Think about how people who want to sell their homes can find you. You should have signs in every location in your target area that has a bulletin board—churches, day care facilities, grocery stores, and faculty lounges at schools. Other good locations include nursing homes and beauty parlors. Self-storage facilities are good places for your signs because many of the tenants are facing some sort of residence change through death, divorce, or layoff.

Your signs should be printed on colored, letter-size paper, in a font large enough to read from 10 feet away but still leaving plenty of *border* around your message. That border is also called *white space*. It attracts more attention than filling a page with text. Here is an example.

> I buy fixer-uppers.
> 555-1234

Twice a month, change your sign for one with a different color of paper. That way, it will keep attracting people's attention.

Resist the urge to put too much information on the sign. Your sign should not do any selling. It should generate a phone call from a prospect who fits your flipping strategy. You can do the selling in person or over the phone. Possible sign messages could include your phone number and one of the following phrases.

- I buy 10–20-year-old houses in need of TLC.

- Sell your home quickly. No need to fix it up or clean it up.
- Quick cash for older homes.
- Be my partner to flip your home.

You want to attract people who just do not want to fool with all the work necessary to make a house ready for sale. Most of them know they are going to take a hit on the sales price, but they do not care. They want the house sold, they want it done with a minimum of hassles, and they do not want to have to worry about it any more.

Can I find properties simply by reading the home sale magazines?

Yes, it can indeed be that simple. Just because a strategy seems obvious does not mean everyone else in the world is following it, competing with you. In my own relatively small community, though, the home sale magazine is filled with many hundreds of properties. All you have is a tiny snapshot of each and about ten words of description. It is a lot to sort through to find that perfect house for a flip and may end up just wasting a lot of your time.

The trick is to work efficiently. When I lived in Houston, I regularly shopped at Niemann Marcus. Their normal prices were way above my income level, but I had a strategy. Once a month I went to the women's wear department, headed straight to the 75%-off sale rack, and did not look at anything else in the store. Yes, there were other sale racks all around. I am sure that many had beautiful clothing at prices I could afford. It did not matter, though, because I wanted only one outfit a month, and I wanted it at 75% off. As a result, I did not waste any time looking at hundreds of dresses and suits, trying on a dozen or so, and then attempting to choose the best one for my purchase.

You should do the same thing. Race through the home sale

magazines looking for these key phrases: *starter home, handyman special,* or *needs TLC.* These phrases all indicate that the homes are fixer-uppers. Clues to owners who need a quick sale at some price include: *motivated seller* and *owner relocated.* Also look for OBO, which means *or best offer.* If you saw an advertisement that said, "$89,000 OBO," would it even occur to you to offer the full asking price of $89,000? Of course not. That owner is just begging for a low offer.

Is there a public version of the Multiple Listing Service that professionals use?

Fortunately, you can gain access to a pared-down version of the MLS (Multiple Listing Service) database upon which many real estate agents rely. Almost all large residential real estate companies have links on their websites to the local MLS. You can search the database by school district, neighborhood, price limit, etc. You can also visit the consumer website for the National Association of Realtors® at **www.realtor.com** and search its MLS database. Even if you cannot easily find flip properties on MLS, you can find properties that fit your purchase profile except for the price. Those are the homes you should track in order to stay in touch with market values.

What homes should I avoid?

Do not buy in neighborhoods with large numbers of houses already on the market. There is too much competition, which usually ends in a price war.

Think long and hard before buying a house that smells bad. It could be pet urine that has soaked into the woodwork and can be eradicated only by ripping out the wood. Damp musty smells could be from a type of older construction that used absorbent materials to clad the outer walls of a house. Over the years the materials soak up moisture from the air like a sponge, and develop a bad odor. You will never get that smell out, unless you remove the cladding.

I do not like to buy from proud homeowners who like to show off their do-it-yourself projects. Usually the work is poorly performed or not up to code, and I am going to end up spending far more money than I planned.

For flippers, it is usually a bad idea to buy houses in historic districts or in subdivisions with strong architectural review committees. The reasons are the same—other people control your fate, they can be totally unreasonable, and they can delay approval for many months.

One friend of mine bought such a house, despite many warnings. His project was delayed one year over disputes concerning things like replacing some of the support piers. The piers were under the house and not seen by the public. He wanted to use concrete block. The historic district board wanted 100-year-old antique brick. He offered to compromise by facing antique brick over concrete block. They wanted antique brick for all of the work. This was just one example of all the problems he suffered. Eventually he remodeled the house, but it was three times more expensive than planned and took over two years.

I do not have time to do research. What are easy sources of flip opportunities?

The easy sources will have the most competition from other potential flippers. You might have to pay a higher price as a result, with a smaller profit margin. On the plus side, though, you can work efficiently and perform more flips than if you had to spend a long lead time to find each one.

The easiest way to find flips is to concentrate on creditor auctions and real estate owned by creditors. That means foreclosures, tax sales, IRS seizures, and similar things. The owner is motivated to sell, needs to sell quickly, and is not as price sensitive as normal people.

Buying property at, or immediately before, foreclosure is a

common type of flip. You need to be careful, though, because you could be purchasing title problems—other people might have superior rights to the property and you could lose your entire investment. In addition, borrowers in many states have the right to buy their property back after a foreclosure, even if an innocent third party owns the home at that time. This is called a *right of redemption*.

While none of the foreclosure issues are particularly tricky, there are a lot of things to learn for this specialty. I suggest you buy a book devoted to foreclosure sales. I have two books you can read: *How to Make Money on Foreclosures* and *The Make Money on Foreclosures Answer Book*.

What happens at a foreclosure?

On the day of the foreclosure sale, a representative of the lender will stand on the courthouse steps and announce that the auction is proceeding. Most of the time, he or she will be the only person present. Sometimes there is a small group of interested bidders. The lender's representative will then usually read the foreclosure ad and ask for bids. Even if it is pouring down rain and no one else is present, the representative will look around expectantly. After a few seconds, he will announce what is called the *credit bid*. That is the amount the lender agrees to credit the loan in return for receiving a deed. There might be other bids, or there might not. The auctioneer announces the winning bidder and the sale price. Then everyone goes back to the office, where people prepare deeds and exchange money.

Even if you are not yet ready to buy any particular property, start going to local foreclosure sales or other creditor auctions. You will gain a sense of the players involved and the local etiquette regarding how things are done. This is all good information to know before it becomes real for you with your own purchase

Is it better to wait and buy after the foreclosure auction?

Whether it is better for you to buy at auction or after the auction depends on your personal goals and restrictions. The deepest discounts and the best bargains usually go to buyers who bid at the auctions. Those buyers also have the greatest risks of the following things.

1. The foreclosure was defective in some manner and the borrower will be able to set it aside.

2. The buyer overlooked one or more title defects, did not purchase title insurance, and someone else can take the property away from the purchaser without paying any money.

3. In some states, the former owner might be able to exercise his or her right to buy the property back from the successful bidder, resulting in the bidder being unable to resell the property for some time period.

4. The former owner can file for bankruptcy and undo the foreclosure sale.

These risks are all manageable, but they can add significantly to your stress level. Risks 1 and 4 can be managed with a buy-back agreement between the buyer and the lender, in the event the foreclosure is contested or set aside in bankruptcy. Good title insurance will take care of Risk 2. As long as you know the redemptory rights in your state, Risk 3 might not exist at all, or you might just have to factor a holding period into your flipping plans.

Buying after the foreclosure auction usually means you must wait some period of time during which the property can be sold only for its appraised value. This might be due to internal lender require-ments or government regulations in the event of a U.S. Department of Housing and Urban Development (HUD) foreclosure. During that time period, real estate agents will successfully sell some of the properties. That means the pool of available deals will be smaller. You will have fewer choices, but they should be safer ones than those up for bidding at foreclosure.

How do I find post-foreclosure properties?

Many post-foreclosure properties will be listed in your local home sales magazine. They usually have the word "foreclosure" promi-nently displayed in the ad. That is because most people who see that word will think the offered price is a deep discount. Those people would be mistaken. The offered price is usually the appraised value.

One word of caution is in order, though. *Appraised value* might mean a full-blown evaluation by a licensed appraiser. It might also mean a drive-by appraisal by a licensed professional made with the assumption that there is nothing wrong with the interior of the house. That assumption is often wrong. A property with a drive-by appraised value of $169,000 might have been appraised at $89,000 if the person driving by knew that the interior had been gutted. Finally, many lenders obtain something called a *broker price opinion*. That is a real estate broker's opinion of the value after driving by the property.

That being said, where else can you find such properties? The easiest source is the Internet. I suggest you start with **www.hud.gov/ homes/homesforsale.cfm**. This site has links for single-family homes and multi-family foreclosure properties owned by HUD, as well as other government agencies and private sources. You might also want to check out some of the commercial sites. Most offer a free trial period, after which you must pay a subscription fee.

Examples of these websites include:
- www.foreclosurelistings.com
- www.foreclosure.com
- www.foreclosurefreesearch.com

How much should I offer?

You will have to start with how much the house will be worth when you are ready to sell it. Then you work backward to calculate your opening offer, and also the highest price you would be willing to pay. The questions that follow will walk you through the process. Here is an example, so you can see the big picture.

An elderly widow in your neighborhood will be moving to another city to live with her daughter. She would like to sell her house quickly so she can use the money to remodel her daughter's two-car garage into an efficiency apartment. Her home is fundamentally sound, but all the finishes are outdated, the appliances need to be replaced, the hedges should be trimmed dramatically, and the house has no central air conditioning despite typical summer temperatures in the high 90s.

You estimate it will cost you $30,000 to completely update the house, throw out the old furnace, and install central heat and air conditioning. Similar homes typically sell for $229,000. If everything goes according to plan, you can complete the remodeling in three months and then sell the house within three months after that.

According to your best estimates, *holding costs* (taxes, insurance, utilities, and interest) will cost you $1,000 per month. You plan to offer an open listing and pay 4% of the sale price to any broker who brings the buyer to the closing table. Your share of closing costs to purchase and sell will amount to $2,000.

This is what the calculations would look like if you wanted to break even. Breaking even is not your goal, of course, but we have to start with that and then work backward to your offer.

Sales price	$229,000
Minus closing costs	–$2,000
Minus sales commission	–$9,160
Minus holding costs	–$6,000
Minus remodeling expenses	–$30,000
Maximum purchase price to break even	$181,840

If the market is soft and it takes six months after completion to sell the house, your holding costs will increase to $9,000. In addition, repairs might be more expensive than originally calculated, so you decide to add a 10% contingency factor and increase that number to $33,000. Now, you have to buy the house for $175,840 in order to break even.

How much profit do you want to make on this flip? If you must make $15,000 in order to make it worth your while, you subtract that number from the $175,840 break-even figure to obtain $160,840. That is the new maximum price you are able to pay for this home. Deduct another several thousand dollars to arrive at your first offer, which gives you some room to negotiate, which should be around $156,000 in this example.

Should I obtain an appraisal for all properties before I buy?

In a perfect world, you would have enough money and enough time to obtain an *appraisal*—a licensed professional's opinion regarding the value of property. A house appraisal will usually cost several hundred dollars and take a few weeks to complete. You can closely duplicate the same appraisal process the professionals use, however. The procedures are fairly simple. They are not very time-consuming because you will be able to use much of the same information you already obtained when looking for flip opportunities.

How do I estimate value?

One way to estimate the *fair market value* (FMV) of a property is to look at sales of similar properties that sold recently. As a flipper, you will need to do this twice. The first time, you will evaluate the comparable sales for your prospective property in its current condition—taking into account physical and legal problems. The second time, you must estimate the value of the house after you buy it and do whatever you have to do for an ultimate sale.

The underlying philosophy of the comparables approach to value is that buyers are indifferent to minor details and will pay the same amount of money for roughly similar properties. You would look at *comparable properties—comps* for short—and then adjust their sale prices upward or downward depending on how they compare relative to your own prospective flip.

As an example, let us assume there have been several recent sales of 3-bedroom, 3-bath brick homes on $1/4$ acre lots, within walking distance of an elementary school in a good school district. They are listed in the following chart, along with differences among the homes.

Form: Comparable Home Sales Analysis				

Date: _____

Comparable #1 address: _____

Comparable #2 address: _____

Comparable #3 address: _____

My property address:_____

Question	#1	#2	#3	Mine
Asking price	$125,000	$100,000	$105,000	$120,000
Actual sales price	$109,000	$98,000	$101,000	
Approximate square feet	1,200	1,100	1,100	1,250
Lot/Land size	1/4 acre	1/4 acre	1/4 acre	1/4 acre
Age of house	30	30	30	30
Age of roof	new	10	12	10
Exterior: brick, wood, etc.	Brick	Brick	Brick	Brick
# bedrooms	3	3	3	3
# bathrooms	2	2	2	2
Quality of finishes*	Budget	Budget	Budget	Budget
Garage/carport/nothing	Carport	Carport	2-car	2-car
Fenced backyard	Yes	No	Yes	No
Condition: excellent/good/ fair/poor	Excellent	Good	Good	Poor

*"Finishes" are the finishing touches that personalize a home. What is the quality of the carpet, cabinetry, wood trim, doors, countertops, wallpaper, lighting fixtures, and plumbing fixtures?

As you can see, your house is most like the first comp, except for the fenced backyard. Fencing a yard is a very inexpensive way to add value to a home. It is also very easy to estimate costs, which are generally done on a dollar-per-running-foot basis. Your roof is ten years old, but the first comp has a new roof. Will that affect value? These are all

3-bedroom, 2-bath starter homes that will not be owned for a long period of time by any one family. As long as the roof has enough life left in it for the next owner, people generally do not care about its age.

The second and third comp houses are virtually identical, except one has a garage and one has only a carport. The one with the garage sold for $3,000 more than the one that had only a carport. A garage is a very important feature for most homeowners, so the garage alone probably added $3,000 worth of value. We can use that information when estimating a value for your home.

As you can see from the chart, your house and the first comp are almost the same, except that yours is in poor condition and has a garage that the comp house lacks. Let us disregard the poor condition for the time being because you plan to fix up your house so it will be in excellent condition, also. After you do that, the only difference between your house and the first comp house will be the garage. We have already determined that a garage adds about $3,000 to the value of a home. If House #1 sold recently for $109,000, then your house—fixed up—should sell for $112,000.

Estimating value is that simple. You might have more points of difference, some of which will cause upward adjustments and some of which will cause downward adjustments in the estimate of your home's value. Just do like the professional appraisers and take each difference in its turn, calculating how much of an increase or decrease in value each causes. Then you do the simple arithmetic at the end to arrive at your own estimate of value.

When I am comparing property sales, what features affect value?

The trick for you is to decide what a minor detail that should be disregarded is, and what something that might affect price and therefore value is. There is no right answer to these questions. It all depends on what type of person is a likely candidate for that particular property, and what features might be important to that person.

In the example for the prior question, our most likely buyer is a young couple with one or two small children or plans to start a family. They are probably on a restricted budget and more focused on functionality than decorative touches. If any of the homes had the following features, I probably would not count them as adding to the value.

- Fireplace
- Crystal chandelier in the living room
- Hardwood floors
- Ceramic tile countertops
- Mature trees

You can certainly argue that some or all of them improve the quality of life or pose potential risks to young children. However, the new parents would not pay extra to acquire those features.

Talk to local real estate agents about features that appeal to particular buyer profiles. Experienced agents will have a good sense of those details and be happy to share them with you. After all, the agent wants to establish credibility with you, so you will be motivated to buy a house they have listed. Be sure to talk to several agents, though. One broker with several corner-lot houses for sale might be convinced that corner-lot houses are important to home buyers. It would be good to get a different point of view on that subject before making your own decisions.

Is there a way to find out the actual sales prices for houses so I can evaluate the comparables?

Real estate agents with access to the full MLS database can generally find out the actual selling prices of property. That is because they share the information with each other via MLS as their properties go to the closing table. If you are working with an agent to find potential flips, he or she can supply you with that information.

Going solo—without an agent—just means you will have to work a little bit harder. If your local government real estate records are online, that is the easiest way to get the information. The officer who records deeds and other real estate instruments will often show the sales price on the face of the document or in the notes. In some places, people who prepare deeds must state the sales price within the body of the deed. Another possibility is to check with the property tax assessor's office—it might have the information you need.

What are holding costs, and how much can I expect to pay?

Holding costs are the expenses you incur just because you own a property, without any outlay for remodeling or repairs. When you calculate your holding costs on a per-month basis, you become keenly aware of the need for urgency in finding a buyer. Every extra month you own the house, that much money is coming out of your pocket. Sometimes, that knowledge will motivate you to take a lower offer from a current prospect rather than wait for something higher from someone who has not even made an appearance yet.

Sample holding costs include:

- the interest on your loan;
- the interest your down payment would have earned if it were still in the bank or other investment;
- utilities;

- insurance premiums;
- real estate taxes attributable to your period of ownership;
- lawn care;
- snow removal;
- pool maintenance;
- pest control; and,
- security system monitoring.

What is the best way to present my offer?

All offers should be presented in writing, preferably on a form that can be easily signed by the seller in order to create a binding contract. Include a short letter containing your most persuasive arguments regarding why this is a good offer. Do not get too wordy. There is no need to explain your entire flipping strategy and market research. Compare the two letters that follow, and see which offer you would choose if you wanted to sell your home in a hurry.

Letter A

Dear Mrs. Evans:

I am a real estate investor who makes money flipping houses like yours. As you know, your home was quite lovely at one time but now suffers from a large amount of deferred maintenance. I think I can make it beautiful again, but the process will be lengthy and expensive. All of those costs and that time seriously affect the value of your home in its current condition. As a result, the most I can offer you is $156,000, but I believe this is a very fair offer. If you agree, please sign the attached contract and return it to me within 24 hours. After that, my offer will expire.

OR,

Letter B

Dear Mrs. Evans:

Thank you for giving me the opportunity to visit your home. I enjoyed talking with you and learning about how you and your late husband built the house with your own hands, over forty years ago. I know it makes you sad that you have not been able to keep it up since his death five years ago. I truly believe that after I restore it, I can find that perfect someone who will cherish it as much as you have. Because of that, I am prepared to offer you the very fair price of $156,000, which is comparable to what similar properties are bringing in our community. Please sign the attached contract at your earliest convenience, but at least by Friday, when I have to make a choice between your home and another purchase.

Letter B is far more likely to get results than Letter A. It is softer, more inclusive, and recruits the seller to buy into your plans for the future. Most importantly, it communicates that other homes in similar condition are selling for comparable prices. Make sure you have the facts to back up that statement if you make it, but that should not be very difficult.

Even if the seller is represented by a real estate agent, still write the cover letter. You will simply give the letter and your contract offer to the agent, who will then pass them along to the seller.

Do I need a contract form, or can I use the one that real estate agents use?

You will need your own contract form, although you can modify one used by other people instead of reinventing the wheel. Most local Associations of Realtors® do have a suggested contract form for their members. It will usually comply with all state laws regarding disclosures. The forms are typically very even-handed because real estate agents use the same form—with situational modifications—when they represent sellers and when they represent buyers. Every company changes the form a little bit, though, to reflect their experiences and concerns. If you can find one to use as an example, it is at the very least a good checklist of what you should include in your own agreement.

If the property is a fixer-upper, do I need a home inspection clause in the contract?

Yes, yes, yes, always yes! For example, a friend of mine bought a small fixer-upper office building years ago. The building was only ten years old, but was in sad shape because the former owner never fixed, painted, or replaced anything. My friend was a very sophisticated investor, and he had firm contracts from subcontractors and suppliers for all the renovation work. He thought he had all his bases covered and did not need to pay for an inspection. He closed without any problems, made all the repairs within budget, raised the rents, and soon filled the office building to 100% occupancy with new tenants. Then one of them needed some additional electrical wiring for an air conditioner in a dedicated computer room. To make a long story short, that is when my friend, and the local government authorities, found out that the building's electrical work did not meet code requirements. In fact, it had never met code. There was talk of the former owner passing some money under the table to a former building inspector.

What did my friend do? He did what he was ordered to do by the inspections department. All his tenants had to vacate the property. All the electrical work had to be ripped out and redone. When it was completed, he had to find new tenants because the old ones had already found new space. A few hundred dollars for an inspection would have saved him all that grief.

What is the normal earnest money amount?

First, earnest money is not required in order to make a binding contract. If you and the seller sign the agreement without making any more changes, you have a contract. Whether or not there is earnest money is irrelevant. If the contract calls for earnest money, but you as the buyer never write the check for some reason, you still have a legally enforceable agreement.

Earnest money serves two functions. It is some indication of your financial ability to close because you at least have on hand the cash for the earnest money. Next, it has hostage value in case you default. Many contracts say that if the buyer defaults, the seller can keep the earnest money but cannot sue for additional damages. Most form contracts created by real estate associations say that if the buyer defaults, the seller and the seller's agent will split the earnest money 50/50.

The typical earnest money amount will vary from community to community. There are no specific rules. One of my clients purchased $650,000 worth of real estate on $5,000 in earnest money. Another client sold $795,000 worth of real estate on $100,000 of earnest money. I have bought property with absolutely no earnest money. You have to evaluate each situation yourself. I would recommend starting out low. If you have identified a good flip opportunity that you can buy cheaply, that is probably because the seller does not have a long line of people waiting to purchase the property. Offer $500 in earnest money and see if the seller counteroffers by demanding more or if he or she is willing to do a deal on that basis.

I would like to specify seller financing in my offer. Does that require any special language?

Reread the prior chapter on financials. It is not enough to simply agree that the seller will hold the financing in some amount. You must also include in your contract the most common terms any borrower and lender would negotiate. At a minimum, you should spell out the interest rate, the term of the loan, how often payments must be made, the amount of the payments, and that the property will stand as security for the loan. If you are buying the property in the name of a corporation or a limited liability company, the seller might want to include something that requires your personal guarantee for the loan. If not, you should not volunteer to guarantee the loan.

In the contract, give yourself time to review the formal note and mortgage or deed of trust after they are prepared. The worst thing you can do is have a short deadline for closing, such as thirty days, and spend the whole time haggling over details of the note and mortgage. When day number thirty comes and goes, you will be in default and the seller could cancel the contract.

Avoid that problem by including a contingency such as the following: "Buyer and Seller will have twenty-one days after contract signing to agree on the exact wording of the note and security documents to be executed at closing. If they are unable to agree by that time, Buyer may extend the closing date an additional twenty-one days in order to secure third-party financing, or Buyer may cancel the contract and receive a refund of the earnest money, or the parties may negotiate for an extension of the closing date, but with all other contract terms and conditions the same." With this language, you at least have a Plan B in case everything falls apart over technicalities of the seller financing.

What can I do to make my offer more attractive to a seller?

In many states, real estate agents who represent sellers are required to give their clients an estimate of closing costs and net sale proceeds.

This must be done at the same time the offer is communicated by the agent to the seller. Even in states with that requirement, though, the agent does not always do a good job of estimating the costs.

For best results, I like to estimate the total closing costs myself. Any closing company can help educate you on how to do this. I then make my offer a little lower than it would otherwise be because I also offer to pay all closing costs. That way, the seller knows that the offer is the amount he or she will put in his or her pocket, except for easy-to-calculate real estate commissions.

Speaking of real estate commissions, you should also address this subject in your offer if the seller is represented by a broker. In all likelihood, the seller signed a contract agreeing to pay the broker a certain percentage of the sale price, usually 6%. But, the broker usually has to split that with whatever broker brings the buyer to the closing table. In reality, the listing broker expected to earn only 3% on his or her listing agreement. If you are not working with a broker or agent, you can specify in your offer that the seller will pay a 3% commission to his or her agent.

If the seller's agent agrees to the reduced commission amount, you can usually make a deal on that basis. If you offered $156,640 for a home, the seller would have to pay the agent $9,398.40 at a 6% commission. But, with only 3% in commissions, the seller saves $4,699.20! That could be the difference between accepting your offer and rejecting your offer.

Can I cancel a contract if my due diligence reveals the flip will not work?

You can withdraw your offer at any time until the seller accepts it and communicates that acceptance to you. Many states have something peculiar called the *mailbox acceptance rule*. It says that if you typically communicate via the mail, and someone accepts your offer by sending you something in the mail, you cannot withdraw your offer after he or she has mailed you his or her acceptance. In other words, giving the acceptance to the post office is the same as giving it to you. Many states have modernized the rule to include emails, so that as soon as a person hits "send" on his or her email accepting an offer, it is the same as if you received it, even if your server is down for several days.

If you indeed have a contract, the question is whether you can cancel it or not if the economics of the deal change.

Most contracts prepared by local real estate associations provide a deadline for a home inspection, and perhaps another one for cancellation based on seller disclosures. Commercial real estate contracts often have many pages of deadlines for inspections, permitting, architectural review, and the like, with the seller having the ability to cancel at any stage. Instead of all that, I typically use an all-purpose due diligence clause. It says I have a certain amount of time to check on anything I want. At the end of that time, I have to go forward to closing or cancel the contract. I can cancel for any reason. This would be a good clause for you to use in your contracts, also.

Are there any technical requirements for canceling a contract?

Some real estate contracts spell out the manner in which they can be canceled. They might say: "On or before thirty days from the Effective Date of this contract, Buyer may cancel for any reason by giving Notice to Seller." That seems straightforward, until you wonder, "What is the Effective Date?" Is it a certain date, or is it the date the last person signed the contract? What was that date? Is there any particular way I have to give notice? One clue is that the word "Notice" is capitalized. That means some other part of the contract defines the word *notice*. Usually, some clause near the end will say that notice is effective if, for example, it is mailed to the recipient by United States Postal Service certified mail, return receipt requested. You have to follow the requirements exactly in that case. You cannot send the notice by Federal Express, for example, just because you believe the seller will receive it more quickly that way.

What happens if the seller accepts my offer?

I suggest a short celebration that night and then straight to work the next day. Make sure you have your financing in order. Finalize any of those arrangements that are not already nailed down. Ask your lender to recommend an approved closing company. Also ask for a copy of the lender's closing checklist. This is routinely given only to the closing company, but that is because of habit, not because of any secrecy. It is good for you to have a copy also, so you can shepherd the closing process through. The checklist usually includes the need to collect a lot of information that either you or the seller already has. Many, many closing delays could be avoided entirely if buyers obtained copies of the closing checklist.

Make appointments for all necessary professionals—home inspector, appraiser, possibly a surveyor. This is also a good time to have any subcontractors and suppliers finalize their prices for you.

Talk to the closing company, and tell them you want owner's title insurance in the amount of your anticipated sale price. *Title insurance* covers you in case the seller did not have good title and there are other claimants to your property. Usually, the closing company writes a lender's policy that protects only the lender. In other words, if you pay $20,000 down, and the bank loans $80,000 for a property, the title insurance company will pay off only $80,000 if it turns out the IRS really owns the home. You are out of luck on your down payment, unless you also have an owner's policy.

Some closing companies will explain all of this to you. Some will not. Even with good intentions, though, they will usually advise you to buy title insurance in an amount equal to the loan and your down payment. They do not think about any extra money you might be spending out of your own pocket, plus all the *sweat equity* you will be putting into the deal. In our prior example, if you completed the renovation of the home, and then the IRS seized it because of a tax lien against the prior owner, how much insurance do you want? Enough to let you break even or enough to equal what you would have sold the house for?

Obtain proof of property and casualty insurance for the closing company. If you are doing any remodeling, you might be required to obtain builder's risk insurance and a separate liability policy. For minor projects, you might be covered with the standard property owner's policy. On the other hand, the normal property owner's policy has outrageously high premiums for vacant houses. If you do not disclose that the house is vacant, you might discover too late that theft and vandalism, for example, are not covered under the circumstances. Find out what is required under the circumstances, bind coverage, and send proof of coverage to the closing company.

Ask your lender for a written estimate of its closing costs. Give it to the closing company, and ask the company to prepare an estimated settlement sheet for you, showing all closing costs and expenses, and also showing how much money you will need to bring to the closing table. Inquire about its policies for that money. In small towns, you can often bring a personal check. Others might require certified funds or a wire transfer of money into the closing company's account.

Finally, go over your post-closing schedules. Are all repair people lined up? Will utilities be switched into your name without any interruption of service? Your carpenter cannot work without electricity. What about dumpsters and port-a-potties, if required? Have them delivered the day after closing, if needed. Cleaning crews, landscapers, and suppliers with specially ordered materials need to be put on notice. One of my friends confided last week that his flip project will be delayed two months while he waits for windows to be delivered. Do not let this happen to you, just because you forgot to check delivery times.

What can I expect at closing?

If you have ever purchased a home of your own, closing on your flip will be substantially the same. The seller will sign the deed and will also sign other documents indicating there are no known title problems, there are no unpaid bills for home repairs, and he or she is not a foreign seller subject to IRS withholding on the purchase money. Both of you will sign documents indicating your understanding that the closing attorney is not *your* attorney and is not obligated to look out for your best interests or give you advice. You will both sign the settlement statement, showing that you agree with the calculations and the distribution of the money. You will sign a promissory note for any financing and a mortgage or a deed of trust, depending on your state.

You will be given a closing packet with copies of all your documents. The lender will receive the original promissory note. The closing company will send the original deed and mortgage to the proper authorities for recording in the real estate records, or it will take the appropriate actions for counties that use the *Torrens system* of real estate registration.

You should make one copy of the closing statement and put it in the accounting file for that flip. Some closing expenses are deductible in the year of purchase. Others must be deducted in a pro rata manner over the lifetime of your loan, with any balances deducted in full if the loan is paid off early. Still, other expenses are added to your *basis*—purchase price—and have the effect of reducing your taxable profit. These rules are different from the ones for deducting expenses associated with buying a primary residence, or even a secondary residence. For the most part, closing expenses for a flip are added to basis, and may not be deducted as business expenses.

Chapter 4

OPTIONS

- What is an option?
- If a seller agrees to give me an option to buy his or her property, can I require that the money I pay for the option be used as a credit against the purchase price?
- Can you give an example of an option contract?
- Do I need a real estate license to buy and sell options?
- How much should I pay for an option?
- How can I avoid two sets of closing costs?
- Where can I find an option contract form?
- What happens if I cannot find a buyer for the property?
- Why wouldn't a potential buyer simply wait until my option expires, and then buy the property at the cheaper price?

What is an option?

An option is a contract. An owner of land—called the *optionor*—agrees to sell his or her land to a particular buyer—called the *optionee*—for a predetermined price. The optionee/buyer is not obligated to buy, though. He or she holds all the cards. The optionor/seller must sell if the other party demands it. The optionee/buyer does not have to buy, no matter how much the owner wants to sell. The buyer makes no promises at all.

Because of technicalities having to do with contract law theories, the optionee/potential buyer must pay a fee to the optionor/seller in order to make the option contract enforceable in most states. The fee does not have to be in any particular amount or any proportion to the ultimate purchase price. It just has to be an amount the owner finds acceptable. The fee is a payment just for the option. The fee does not pay for the property, nor is it earnest money or a down payment. The optionor gets to keep the payment regardless of whether the optionee buys the property or not.

If a seller agrees to give me an option to buy his or her property, can I require that the money I pay for the option be used as a credit against the purchase price?

No. What you are describing is *earnest money*. If you try to make the money you pay for the option refundable, or capable of being applied against the purchase price, then you do not have an enforceable option contract. Do not try to figure out any way to wiggle around this! If you are serious about using options to invest, then be serious about making sure you can enforce the contract when the seller finds out his or her property is much more valuable than he or she originally thought.

Can you give an example of an option contract?

This is how a typical option contract works.

> Stephen inherited his parents' home and uses it for rental income. Mary Jo knows that Stephen would sell the house if he could receive $129,000 for it, but most buyers want to live in the house. Stephen needs the rental income, so he cannot afford to kick out the tenant while he markets the house for a sale. Stephen could put a clause in his lease allowing him to cancel the lease if he finds a buyer, but that would scare away many tenants. Stephen has a problem he does not know how to solve. Mary Jo knows an investor who might be interested in buying the house and who would be willing to pay $159,000.
>
> Mary Jo has three problems: (1) she has no cash for a down payment; (2) she does not have the ability to borrow money for purchase and holding costs; and, (3) she has no experience managing tenants.
>
> It is November, though, and Stephen would like some extra cash for the holidays. Mary Jo says to Stephen: "I will pay you $500 right now if you will sign a contract giving me the right to buy your property any time during the next six months for $129,000. The $500 is yours to keep, no matter what happens. But, if you change your mind about selling and want to refund the $500 and cancel the contract, you will not be allowed to do that. If I decide not to buy, I will have no obligation to you, but you still keep the $500."
>
> If Stephen agrees, Mary Jo will have six months to use her superior contacts, knowledge, and hard work to find a buyer willing to pay the more realistic fair market value of $159,000. She can buy the house and then resell it the same day, or she can simply sell her option to the buyer. Mary Jo will never have

her name on the title, she will not go through a closing, and she will have no sale expenses.

At the end, she will make a return of $29,500 on a cash investment of only $500! Of course, she might not be able to pull it off. If she fails, she loses her $500, but no more. This type of risk can be managed easily by most people.

Do I need a real estate license to buy and sell options?

In some states, you might need a real estate license to buy and sell options. A sample license law says: "It shall be unlawful for any person, partnership, corporation, or branch office, for a fee, commission, or other valuable consideration, or with the intention or expectation of receiving or collecting a fee, commission, or other valuable consideration from another, to do any of the following unless he or she is licensed ... Buy or sell or offer to buy or sell, or otherwise deal in options on real estate..."

Use Appendix E to find the contact information for the real estate licensing authority in your state. Ask someone there if you will need a license for your option flipping strategy.

How much should I pay for an option?

How much you pay for an option will depend on: (1) the lowest amount the owner will accept; and, (2) the largest amount of money you can afford to gamble if you cannot find a buyer. Remember, the money you pay for an option is not refundable.

How can I avoid paying two sets of closing costs?

Put a clause in the option contract giving you the right to assign the option to someone else if you choose. That person then goes through with closing with the owner. In the example at the beginning of this chapter, Mary Jo paid $500 for an option on a house.

With an assignment clause, she could then sell her option to someone else for $30,000. That person would then have the right to buy the real estate from Stephen for $129,000, or a total cash outlay of $159,000. That was the same amount the buyer was willing to pay, anyway. There is only one closing, one set of closing costs, and Mary Jo is never even in the chain of title. This is especially important if Mary Jo has creditors trying to seize any real estate she might own.

Where can I find an option contract form?

You should consult with a local attorney. State laws vary widely, so I do not recommend using a generic form from the Internet.

What happens if I cannot find a buyer for the property?

If you do not go through with the purchase, you lose the money you paid to buy the option. That is all. Nothing worse happens to you.

Why wouldn't a potential buyer simply wait until my option expires, and then buy the property at the cheaper price?

It is always a possibility that a buyer will go around you, find out the details of your arrangement, and then simply wait you out. There is no foolproof way to keep this from happening. As a practical matter, though, it is very rare.

Chapter 5

FIXING UP A HOUSE

- Will I need to hire a contractor to fix up a house?
- What regulatory requirements will I need to meet before beginning repairs or remodeling?
- How do I prepare a budget for a flip?
- Are there any rules of thumb about house repairs?
- How do I choose the right repairs to make?
- Is remodeling too risky for a beginning flipper?
- What finishes will give me the best bang for my buck?
- What repairs do most people overlook when planning a flip?
- How do I prepare a budget for my repairs or renovations?
- In what order does the work need to be performed?
- If I am doing only minor repairs and cleanup, do I need to prepare a budget?
- I'm pretty handy. Can I do the repair work myself?
- I do not know a ball peen hammer from a ball-point pen. Is there anything I can do myself on a repair or remodel flip?
- What is the best way to keep my costs down?
- What are some penalty-type expenses I can avoid?
- On a fixer-upper flip, what would you consider unnecessary expenses?
- How do I get the best prices for my labor and materials?
- Is it safe to buy building materials on eBay?
- Someone recommended buying scratch and dent items. What are they?
- Can I save money buying from builders' salvage stores?

Will I need to hire a contractor to fix up a house?

In most states, a property owner may act as his or her own general contractor. You can find your state's licensing requirements by going to the Craftsman Book Company website at:

www.contractors-license.org

What regulatory requirements will I need to meet before beginning repairs or remodeling?

Regulation requirements can vary widely from community to community. At a minimum, you may be required to obtain a construction permit, even for very minor structural, electrical, or plumbing repairs or renovations. You can go to the Permit Place website at **www.permitplace.com** for more information, although it does not provide an exhaustive list. You should also call your local permit office. Start with your city hall, or your county or parish government if you are not inside city limits, and ask for guidance and other phone numbers. You might have overlapping jurisdictions for requirements, such as:

- inside city limits;
- outside city limits but inside the police jurisdiction;
- outside both, but subject to county/parish rules;
- regional planning, zoning, and permitting authorities; or,
- special "overlay" districts that cover portions of several municipalities.

It is very important to find out the exact requirements because the permitting and the building standard costs could significantly alter your budget.

How do I prepare a budget for a flip?

The best way to estimate house flipping expenses is to begin with a good checklist of expense categories. Start with my sample budget categories, found in Appendix C.

Next, ask subcontractors and suppliers for firm quotes on as many items as possible. For the remainder, use software, experts, or the Internet to calculate probable expenses. Bear in mind that most quotes are good for only thirty days. If there is a significant delay between obtaining the quote and beginning the work, you will need to request an updated quote.

Are there any rules of thumb about house repairs?

You have probably heard the expression, "I'm all thumbs today," meaning someone cannot seem to do anything right. He or she drops things, hits the wrong keys on the computer, and has trouble buttoning a shirt. Nothing seems to work right when you are all thumbs. Rules of thumb are exactly the same thing—trouble waiting to happen.

You might hear that painting will cost you $1 per square foot of house, for example. That does not take into consideration high ceilings, substantial molding and trim work, water-based versus oil-based paints, or the need to protect finished floors. Painting is a messy business. Normally, you schedule painters before the flooring people because of all the drips. But, if you have hardwood floors that do not need refinishing, your painters have to be extra careful. It adds to the cost.

Even fencing, which is normally priced on the basis of number of running feet of fence line, can hold surprises for you. If you have a lot of turns, or your lot is not level, or local restrictions require black or green powder-coated chain link instead of galvanized aluminum, the cost will go up.

All the rules of thumb have the same deficiencies. A rule of thumb should be used for initial screening purposes only. They are extremely valuable for that purpose, so you should learn the rules used in your community. If you are thinking about a house that can be purchased for $75,000 and sold for $150,000, but your rule of thumb says that repairs will cost $75,000, that house is probably a bad investment and you should not spend any additional time on it. On the other hand, if your rule of thumb says the repairs will be only $20,000, then it makes sense to invest the time for a detailed analysis.

How do I choose the right repairs to make?

First, make distinctions in your mind between repairs, remodeling, and finishes. *Repairs* are necessary to restore something to functionality, such as broken toilets, rotten subflooring, and holes in walls. *Remodeling* changes the layout or components of a house, usually by adding or removing walls, cabinets, doors, and windows. *Finishes* are the finishing touches that usually involve decorative choices—carpet, paint, wall-covering, countertops, wood trim, doors, plumbing fixtures, and lighting fixtures.

Repairs should be limited to the following:

- prevention of further damage (roof repairs);
- basic functionality (toilets, holes in surfaces, rotten wood in potentially dangerous places);
- safety issues (electrical up to code requirements); and,
- things that must be revealed by your state's disclosure laws.

If you are thinking about repairs that do not fall into one of those categories, think long and hard about whether they are really necessary. The finished home does not have to be perfect.

Is remodeling too risky for a beginning flipper?

Simple renovations—like changing a few walls or doors—can easily be handled by novices. In fact, they may be essential for upgrading an older home to modern tastes. Years ago, homes had separate rooms for the kitchen, laundry, pantry, informal dining, and family gathering room or den. Today, many of these are more likely to be one large space. If you are flipping an older home, you will probably need to tear out some walls to appeal to today's homeowners. Older homes also tend to lack closets and a sufficient number of bathrooms. You will have to add those, as well. There is no point in telling a prospective purchaser that he or she can buy a beautiful armoire to use as a closet—he or she will just remember that your house has no closets. Bite the bullet and build some.

I generally discourage beginning flippers who want to replace windows. Removing old windows usually reveals rotten wood, poor carpentry that was covered up with layers of caulking, and irregular sizes requiring special orders. If you think the windows absolutely, positively must be replaced, then choose stock replacements that are kept in-store at most home improvement places.

Keep in mind the following story. A friend of mine special-ordered windows for his most recent flip project. The store told him they would be delivered in three weeks, which worked well with his schedule. Three weeks later he called to inquire about the exact date of delivery. The person at the store told him the windows were on back order, with an anticipated ship date two months later. His project is now at a complete standstill, waiting for those windows. Because of taxes, insurance, utilities, and interest, it costs him $5,000 for every month he stands idle. This is not an uncommon occurrence with special orders.

What finishes will give me the best bang for my buck?

Choose finishes that are compatible with the house and with recent sales in your price range.

Starter homes usually have a minimal amount of decorative details, easily cleaned surfaces, and carpet that can hide a multitude of stains. That generally means laminate countertops rather than tile, because cleaning the grout in tile is not a fun thing. Solid surfaces, like granite or Corian, are too expensive for starter homes and require special care. Go for vinyl flooring in the kitchen and bathrooms and oatmeal-colored berber-type carpet in the rest of the house. Look for cabinets with a minimum of details or vinyl laminate surfaces. Single-unit tub and shower enclosures are best. Appliances should be budget quality. Keep light fixtures and plumbing fixtures plain. Spend money fencing the backyard to make a child- and pet-friendly place, and spend a little money landscaping the front yard so it looks like the other ones in the neighborhood. Install vinyl mini-blinds in all windows so potential buyers do not have to think about the cost of window coverings in addition to their home purchase.

Second or third homes for young professionals moving up in their careers must generally reflect some stature and style. The potential buyer feels he or she has worked hard and deserves some nice things and some creature comforts. These potential buyers may require a well-appointed backdrop for business entertaining. Spend your money in the public areas. Put some granite or marble on the entryway floor. Use crown molding in the public areas, good quality vinyl flooring in the kitchen, and laminated flooring that looks like wood in the dining room. Put a fancy light fixture in the dining room, the entry foyer, and at the front stoop. Use decorative plumbing fixtures in the powder room and ceramic tile or stone on that floor. Purchase midrange appliances like Whirlpool, GE

Monogram® series, KitchenAid, or comparable brands. As always, landscape the property in accordance with neighborhood standards.

Luxury homes are not really a good idea for beginning flippers, so I am not going to cover them here. I will point out that even luxury homes cut corners in places not typically noticed by guests. I have gone to open houses for homes priced at $750,000 and up. They look pretty on the surface, but then you see that all closets have wire shelves, rather than solid wood. The windows are usually something called *contractor grade*, which translates to inexpensive. Granite countertops do not include granite back-splashes. The plumbing fixtures are cheap knockoffs of much better quality designer fixtures and the ceiling fans are the $29 ones from the sale bin at the home improvement store, not anything that will last for long. Drawer bottoms are usually very thin plywood, not solid wood, and the drawer glides are lightweight and not full-extension.

Homes that appeal to retirees emphasize comfort, safety, security, convenience, and storage. Spend money on paddle handles instead of door knobs. Plumbing fixtures should also have paddle handles rather than hard-to-grip knobs. Choose a security system that includes a second keypad in the master bedroom. Install grab bars in the master bathroom, carpet in all rooms except the kitchen in order to provide plenty of non-slip surfaces, and use plenty of exterior lighting that can be controlled from the master bedroom and some other location. If possible, put in lazy-Susan corner base cabinets to make good use of space. Anyone over 30 or so simply cannot get down on their hands and knees to rummage around in the standard corner base cabinet.

What repairs do most people overlook when planning a flip?

Unfortunately, it is usually the big ticket items that are overlooked by novice flippers. That includes the need to completely rewire a house, replace some or all of the plumbing lines, and repair or replace HVAC (heating, ventilation, and air conditioning) systems.

Electrical is a common problem because of the building inspection system used in most cities and towns. If you obtain a building permit in order to make minor repairs and renovations, the inspectors are allowed to inspect anything else within eyesight of the areas under repair or renovation. Almost always, an inspector sees something suspicious about electrical wiring and then requires you to bring the entire system up to current code standards. Another route to the same upgrade is when the fire marshal does a fire safety inspection at the completion of your project. If you cannot pass because of electrical deficiencies, you will have to spend additional money.

Finally, many people neglect inspecting the foundation of a house. Especially if it is built on a basement or a crawl space, you may have significant settling issues. That problem can usually be remedied with the installation of supports, but it is not a cheap fix.

To avoid being a sad story in someone's flipping book, be sure to obtain a complete house inspection before your purchase contract becomes final. Before hiring an inspector, make sure he or she will advise you of building code deficiencies, not just things that do not work properly. All the electrical in the house might work perfectly, but that will not help you if you still have to bring it up to code.

How do I prepare a budget for my repairs or renovations?

First, revisit Chapter 2, specifically the questions starting with: "How much will repairs cost?" That chapter deals with estimating expenses on the front end, to see if you want to pursue an opportunity or not. Some people call that process a *back-of-the-envelope pro forma*. It means a very rough estimate of your expenses, potential sales price, and anticipated profit. If you did a full-blown budget on every potential flip you ran across, you would suffer from a disease industry insiders call *analysis paralysis* or sometimes the *getting ready syndrome*.

If you read budgets prepared by experienced flippers, you might see very broad categories of expenses such as "rough electrical" or "finish carpentry." That is probably fine if you do the same type of house all the time and are very comfortable with the kinds of expenses you will encounter. For beginners, I recommend a budget just as detailed as you can make it. There are three reasons for that.

1. It helps to have a checklist to make sure you have not overlooked anything. "Finish carpentry" is fine as a category, but breaking that down into items such as "install crown molding in the dining room" helps you remember that you must cost out the molding itself, and have someone stain or paint it, in addition to just installing it.

2. You have better communication with subcontractors and suppliers because you itemized the things you want.

3. You are able to ask pointed questions, such as: "What have I omitted from this list?" When I first started flipping properties, it came as a shock to me that when you buy a one-piece tub and shower, faucet set, and showerhead, you have to separately buy valves, drain flanges, and other such items.

Materials should all be listed individually, with the cost plus sales tax and delivery fees where relevant. Labor should include firm bids or estimates of man-hours to complete and labor rates per hour. Include time estimates for the completion of various categories of work. This will let you know how long your project will take, and it will let you schedule subcontractors who must do their work in a certain order. If you cannot estimate the time, ask someone at the store where you will be buying the supplies for help with that task. They can usually help you with estimates for time and for labor costs.

Appendix B has a sample budget for you. Be sure to review all items, even if I did not supply a number. The sample budget will be a good checklist for items you need to consider when preparing your own.

In what order does the work need to be performed?

In a nutshell, start at the top of the house and work your way down. There are exceptions, of course. You do not want to finish walls and flooring on the upper levels, and then start adding supports in the basement to level the house. That is a sure recipe for ruining all the other work as walls and floors shift around.

In addition, think about what workers will be in what spaces. You do not want workers getting in each other's way, such as cabinet installers and appliance installers coming on the same day. Avoid scheduling one set of subcontractors that must destroy another's work in order to do their own. An example would be doing the land-scaping first, and then having heavy delivery trucks and workers walk all over it every day. Ask your subcontractors what would make their job easier when it comes to scheduling. An electrical contractor might give you a better price if he or she can do the electrical work before someone else hangs drywall. That is because everything is open and accessible before the drywall goes up. Afterward, the electrician has to fish the walls, and they do not like doing that, so it costs extra.

For most house repair projects, the following is the order of the work.

1. Roof
2. Rough carpentry (including window installation)
3. Finish carpentry
4. Mechanicals—water, power, gas, HVAC
5. Paint and wall-covering
6. Flooring
7. Cabinetry
8. Fixtures—plumbing and electrical
9. Appliances
10. Landscaping

If I am doing only minor repairs and cleanup, do I need to prepare a budget?

I recommend you always prepare a budget, no matter how small the job. It is a good failsafe to make sure you have considered all the potential expenses of a project. Even a housekeeping flip—requiring little more than cleaning the house—has some expenses. You will need a dumpster, for example, or you will need to rent a trailer and haul garbage to the dump. You cannot just put everything in the back of your car and leave it on your curb for your regular trash pickup.

I once did a housekeeping flip for a home that used to belong to a university chemistry professor. He was quite the mad scientist, always whipping up things in his basement. When he died, his family left everything down there, afraid to touch it. Five years later, when I bought the house, strange substances still filled beakers and jars piled everywhere, wall-to-wall and floor-to-ceiling. All the potentially hazardous waste had to be specially handled. It could not be tossed into the dumpster. That added some extra expenses to an otherwise boring project.

Finally, preparing a budget for small jobs does two things for you. It lets you practice on little projects to see how close you come to hitting your numbers. It also gives you credibility when you visit a lender, asking for an acquisition and rehab loan. Lenders are comforted when they know you have actually thought through a project, instead of making up the numbers.

I'm pretty handy. Can I do the repair work myself?

"Pretty handy" around the house is completely different from being able to do a house flip on your own with no subcontractors. I do not want to discourage you, but please start out with a small project containing a limited variety of chores. You will quickly find out that many tasks require two people for safety or logistics reasons. As my husband always tells me, "Someone has to hold the dumb end of the tape measure." If you are going it alone, make sure you have a helper, if only to hold the ladder or call the ambulance.

Think back to all your personal home improvement projects. Did they all take far longer than you thought? Were you required to make several trips to the store to buy more screws, select lumber, or rent specialized tools? Things will not be any different on a house flip. Pick those jobs for which you already have a good supply of extra small parts and fasteners and the specialized tools you are likely to need. For everything else, it is probably cheaper to hire it out and sell the house more quickly than try to do the work yourself and delay a resale.

I do not know a ball peen hammer from a ball-point pen. Is there anything I can do myself on a repair or remodel flip?

You can *demo* things, which is short for demolition or demolish. As long as you avoid support walls necessary for holding up the roof or the upper floors, you can swing a sledge hammer to your heart's content.

If it has to be done, you might as well be the one doing it. It can be fun, you will save money, and you can tell fun stories like all the real construction professionals.

One word of advice, though. Old vinyl tile squares are usually a whole lot harder to remove than you might think. I recommend leaving that work to professionals.

What is the best way to keep my costs down?

There is no one best way to keep down your costs. You should, instead, stay focused on this issue and do everything possible to minimize costs without sacrificing quality. Just like preparing your own personal household budget, you want to think about three areas: (1) avoid penalties that are your own fault—things like late charges on your credit card or overdraft fees on your checking account; (2) do not spend money on things that are not necessary; and, (3) find the best price for things that are necessary.

What are some penalty-type expenses I can avoid?

On a construction site, unnecessary expenses that can be avoided with proper planning and management include the following.

- *Emptying the dumpster too often because workers are allowed to toss bulky items in without any attention to maximizing the fill volume.* In goes a cabinet or two, then some plywood that creates a floor effect, then a few pieces of drywall, and your dumpster is full.

There are several pockets of empty space, but nothing more will fit because of the way the dumpster was filled. You have to pay each time the dumpster is hauled off and emptied. Those dollars can add up pretty quickly.

- *Theft of supplies is a major problem on worksites.* Be sure to lock up absolutely everything at the end of each day. If possible, and if there is not a delivery fee for each trip, have only one day's supplies delivered each day. There is less to lock up at night, it is easier to keep track of materials being used during the day, and it is harder for dishonest workers to steal materials during the day.

- *Over-ordering supplies will usually result in restocking fees if you send unused materials back for a credit.* That is, if you order 7,000 bricks, just to be on the safe side, but you return 2,000 of them, you will usually have to pay a 20% *restocking fee.* In other words, you do not get full credit for a refund on returned items, but only an 80% credit.

- *Be present at the worksite first thing in the morning, and last thing at night, if at all possible.* Make notes regarding who arrives and leaves, and at what times. If work stops for a day or two because of bad weather, note that also. Some subcontractors are simply dishonest and will bill you for time they did not actually work. Drug abuse and alcoholism are also rampant in the trades. Others are simply sloppy, keep poor time records, and then try to reconstruct their hours at the end of the job. You usually get the short end of that stick.

- *On any time-and-materials contract, the owner often ends up paying the contractor to correct his or her own mistakes.* I have had plumbers drop tubs and then charge me for the replacement, carpenters fail to use a level and then charge me to rip out work and start over, and electricians who put lights in wrong places and then bill me for change orders when they had to be moved. The only defense is to have a firm policy of payment only for signed change orders and to be present at the job site as much as possible to catch mistakes. I have had some absolute jewels for general contractors, people I would trust with the password to my bank account, but such people are rare. Constant vigilance will keep down unnecessary costs. Blind faith will not.

On a fixer-upper flip, what would you consider unnecessary expenses?

Any expense that does not pay for itself by adding to the value of the house or allowing it to be sold more quickly is an unnecessary expense.

Here is an example from the beginning of my career, many years ago. In order to provide a real luxury feel to some offices, I covered one wall in each office with wallpaper. It was an accent wall, which was very popular at the time. Not just any wallpaper would do for me because I expected to have very discriminating tenants. As a result, I chose $120-a-roll Italian silk wall covering. One ten-foot wall cost a little over $1,000, and I had many offices with many such walls.

No doubt about it, the walls were exquisite—for a day or two, until the first fingerprints that could not be wiped off the Italian silk. Until the first tenant drove railroad spikes into that silk to hold up a bulletin board. I quickly realized that my tenants did not care about having an Italian silk wall covering, and it was a really stupid thing on which to spend money for a rental space.

Do not make my mistake. Keep in the forefront of your mind all the details of houses in your ultimate price range. The quality of your materials and your selection of features should match those other houses, not what you want in your own dream home. If you feel you must splurge on something to stand out from the crowd, pick one dramatic thing only. I recommend a steam shower. They cost far less than a whirlpool tub and appeal to men and women both. Other possibilities are a hot tub/spa, closed circuit security cameras, or a water feature in the landscaping. When prospective buyers are talking about homes they have visited, you want them to say, "Which one had the steam shower?" I guarantee you that the dramatic statement in one area will overcome economy choices in other areas.

How do I get the best prices for my labor and materials?

The tried and true method for getting the best price is to shop around. Keep track of what everyone charges and any differences in quality. You will be amazed at the wide variations in pricing. Faucets at the plumbing supply place could be twice as much or half as much as at the home improvement superstore. You just cannot take anything for granted, and must constantly compare prices. That is the only way to guarantee that you will always obtain the best prices.

Is it safe to buy building materials on eBay?

As with any purchase from an online auction site, safety depends on the integrity of the seller and on your understanding of what is really being sold. Beyond that, I think online auctions are an excellent way to get wonderful building materials and fixtures at bargain prices.

If colors are important, make sure you know the names of manufacturers' colors and what they look like in the real world. I once had a car in a color called "Fire Mist Faun Metallic." What color is that?

Do you think a computer monitor would do it justice? If sinks came in Fire Mist Faun Metallic, I might have to see a real sink before I ordered one to match my bathroom tile. Home improvement super-stores are terrific places for that research. They always have a lot of different models and even more paint chips for special order items. You can look around yourself, and do not have to feel guilty about wasting a salesperson's time. Just be careful when trying to match colors with online purchases.

Another thing you should know well is model numbers. One digit difference in the model numbers, between something you saw in a store and something you buy online, could mean very dramatic differences in features. Or, it could be something completely mean-ingless, like a newer model microwave with 1,200 watts of power instead of 1,175 watts.

Finally, make sure you know the dimensions of the item you are buying. For appliances, you can usually go to the manufacturer's website to obtain that information, even for older models. Faucet sets generally separate into *center hole* or *two hole* (meaning one control for the water, or separate handles for hot and cold) models and categories depending on the spacing between the holes. This is important if you want to put a new faucet on an existing sink. For light fixtures, you need to know the obvious dimensions, plus the weight. Unless you have a sturdy beam onto which you can screw an electrical box, some fixtures will be too heavy for your ceiling.

When buying wallpaper, make sure all rolls are from the same dye lot; otherwise, the colors on different rolls might not match exactly. Do the same thing with carpet tile squares.

In general, make sure you are buying from a reputable seller, and make sure you know what you are buying. With those two thoughts in mind, happy hunting for online construction materials, and enjoy your significant savings!

Someone recommended buying scratch and dent items. What are they?

Scratch and dent items are exactly as described. Usually appliances or cabinets, they have some sort of cosmetic damage that does not affect functionality. On my last flip, all my appliances had major blemishes on the sides. I did not care, though, because they were all flanked by cabinets or by walls. No one would ever see the defects. I saved about 60% off the normal list prices.

Check with appliance stores and home improvement stores in your area to find out who typically offers scratch and dent merchandise. After that, it is a simple matter to keep track of their sale schedules. With luck, you will find a friendly vendor who agrees to let you store the items in its warehouse, free of charge, until you are ready for installation.

In addition, some stores sell only damaged merchandise. My own mother owned such a store while I was in college, to help pay for college expenses. She purchased items from JC Penney—usually things that had been damaged in shipment. Some she repaired and some she sold "as is," but the buyers always received a large discount.

Can I save money buying from builders' salvage stores?

This is another great idea for saving money. Often, buildings scheduled for demolition will first have all salvageable parts removed. They find their way to salvage stores where they are sold at deep discounts, or to architectural antiques stores, where they cost you an arm and a leg. You can find doors, windows, cabinet hardware, door knobs, light fixtures, and plumbing fixtures, to name a few categories.

Check your sizes, just like shopping online. Inspect everything very carefully for damage, and make sure all working parts actually work. Be especially careful with windows and doors—look for rotten wood, double check all dimensions, and do not buy anything that has to be stripped. I speak from personal experience, having stripped far more woodwork than I care to think about. It always turns out to be a bigger job than you think.

On one flip, I stripped several layers of paint off once-beautiful oak, walnut, and maple. With the end in sight, I ran up against the final layer. It was antique milk paint! That type of paint laughs at ordinary strippers. At the time, I did not know that you could buy a specialized solvent for milk paint. I had no choice but to repaint the woodwork—something I could have done before all that stripping. Yes, the surfaces look much better because I did strip all the old paint. On the other hand, this is one of those areas like my silk-covered walls. Do not waste money stripping down to original wood and then repainting, because no one does it. Your efforts will not be rewarded with a higher sales price, a better comparison with other home choices on the market, or a faster sale.

On the whole, though, builders' salvage stores can represent excellent bargains, saving you 60% to 90% off retail prices for similar items.

Chapter 6

PARTICULAR PROJECTS

- How can I improve the curb appeal of a house?
- I cannot afford a complete kitchen remodel. What are some quick fixes?
- What is the best way to update a bathroom?
- The family room has dark paneling and no windows. What can I do?
- What other quick fixes can I do inexpensively?

How can I improve the curb appeal of a house?

Three words add up to increased curb appeal: cleaning, painting, and landscaping. Of the three, cleaning is easiest and should be tried first before more aggressive strategies. Not only are painting and landscaping more expensive, but you might need to supply detailed plans to an architectural review committee or other community review board. They could have veto power over your choices and could impose expensive requirements of their own.

That is why I recommend starting with a good cleaning. A brick house, or one with vinyl siding, can usually benefit from pressure washing. Pressure washers are so useful that I recommend you buy one rather than rent. You will find yourself using yours to clean vehicles, driveways, outdoor furniture, grills, and decks.

Cleaning a front yard means pruning out-of-control shrubberies and trees, re-sodding bare parts of the lawn, and removing any and all yard art. None of those things should require any committee approval.

The next step up is paint. Nothing dresses up a house faster than a fresh coat of paint. Flipping a house is not the time to go out on a limb with an exciting new color scheme. Stick to fairly traditional colors and color combinations. Look around the neighborhood to see what color schemes are popular and stay within that group.

Finally, changing the landscaping can completely transform a house. You can purchase landscaping software for under $50. I use 3D Garden Composer, which currently retails for $39. I can take digital photographs of my property, import them into the software, and then add a wide variety of plants, outdoor furniture, garden ornaments, fences, decks, walls, and walkways. I can grow my plants over many years to see what they will look like in the future. I can view the sun's shade at different times of the day, and I can change the seasons to see seasonal colors. The software includes an extensive encyclopedia of plants, recommendations for your particular needs, and online ordering of plants to help you prepare a budget.

I cannot afford a complete kitchen remodel. What are some quick fixes?

There is no doubt about it, a kitchen can turn into a black hole, sucking out all your money and demanding more. It is particularly hard for me, because I love to cook and practically live in my kitchen. I assume many people are the same as me and must fight the urge to outfit kitchens with the things I would want. I think that a lot of flippers get into trouble with the same type of problem.

You can update a kitchen without breaking the budget, however. Increasing the size and the natural light are probably the two best strategies if they are possible. Knocking out walls between the kitchen, laundry room, and formal dining room can transform a house. Do not expand the actual kitchen area into the new space—leave it open, to be used in whatever way the new homeowner wants. The extra area could accommodate a family table for meals, homework, and projects. It could be a family room for comfortable seating and a television. It could be a hobby area. The point is to provide open space where families and friends can easily gather, and then let people use their own imaginations.

Natural light also helps. If possible, install a large window that looks out onto a pleasing landscape. Sometimes the house design works against you, though, and the only view is the side of the neighbor's house. In that case, use glass block or some other medium that lets in light, but not the ability to see what is outside. Avoid skylights. They are tricky to install, and I have never had one that did not eventually leak.

If you ripped out a laundry room, create a new one in a laundry closet hidden by louvered bi-fold doors. All you need is enough space for the washer and dryer, with a shelf above for supplies. Sorting and folding can be done in the kitchen itself. I remodeled a farmhouse once, and put a stacked washer and dryer in a former linen closet next to the powder room. When I described what I wanted to do, all my friends were skeptical. Once they saw the setup, everyone agreed it made perfect sense.

Cabinets can be updated easily by replacing only the doors and the drawer fronts and possibly the hinges. Paint everything, install new knobs and pulls, and you are in business. If the shelves and drawer bottoms are unattractive particle board, cover them with shelf liner in a pretty color and pattern.

Put down good quality sheet vinyl flooring in a light color to enhance the open and airy feeling you want. Use laminated counter-tops in a neutral color, preferably with some sort of a small pattern. Right now, a multicolored tweed sort of look is very popular. I do not like to use laminates that pretend to be something else, like granite or walnut. It just reminds me that the counter is a fake. There is nothing wrong with good, honest laminate. It lasts a long time, is inexpensive to replace if you want to redecorate, and it cleans up easily. That is more than I can say for ceramic tile, wood, or granite!

Keep appliance costs down by shopping the scratch and dent sales or buying refurbished appliances. If you can find a refrigerator at a terrific price, it is always a good investment. Not all homes come with one. It could tip the scales for a potential buyer to purchase your home and not have to worry about immediately shopping for a refrigerator.

If you want decorator touches, do it with lighting. Light fixtures are amazingly inexpensive and come in a wide variety of styles and colors. The right fixtures can really punch up an otherwise bland room.

Finally, I like to install a closed circuit television monitor in the kitchen. The four-camera wireless packages are under $500. One camera could show the backyard, one could show the front door, and the two extras could be used where needed—perhaps as a baby-cam or for viewing wildlife. This feature adds a lot of punch, and helps reinforce the kitchen as the command center of the house.

What is the best way to update a bathroom?

Modern homeowners prize space in their bathrooms but generally limit their focus to the master bath. Formerly, a bathroom was entirely functional, with a toilet, sink, and tub crowded into as little space as possible. If at all possible, increase the size by taking over some other room, such as part of a foyer in very old houses with large entries, or possibly splitting an adjacent bedroom into additional bath space and a walk-in closet and dressing room.

If there is no more space, create the illusion of size. Replace the standard sink/cabinet combination with a pedestal sink. Recess shelving into the spaces between wall studs. Think about replacing the tub with a shower enclosure. Provide plenty of lighting, and decorate in light, neutral colors. A wallpaper border at the ceiling will draw the eye upward, away from the clutter, and create the illusion of more space.

Many older homes are bargain purchases because they have only one bathroom. When I was growing up, all my friends lived in three-bedroom, one-bathroom homes. Those homes are still out there, but they are highly undesirable. Adding a second bath can transform the marketability—and sales price—of a house. Rob space from the formal living room or possibly even the garage. My friend Tony converted a one-car garage into a spa—complete with soaking tub, steam shower, and lounge area—for under $5,000. The new owners were happy with a tiny room housing only a sink and toilet in the master bedroom area, because they had a luxury spa on the other side of the house.

Powder rooms are always popular. If the house does not have one, you can create one in space as small as sixteen square feet. Because powder rooms are used infrequently, and usually only by guests, homeowners do not feel the need for spaciousness there.

Aside from these structural considerations, you can update a bathroom in the same manner as a kitchen. Use laminate countertops and sheet vinyl flooring in modern colors and patterns. Hang a framed mirror rather than the typical sheet of mirrored glass. Spend a little extra on light fixtures, but avoid those that require specialty bulbs. You will soon forget about the $20 price tag on a standard light strip, when you must buy five globe light bulbs at $6 each. I also dislike anything that requires candelabra based bulbs. The bulbs are expensive, and it is virtually impossible to find them in the fluorescent, low-wattage versions if you want to save energy.

Replace the toilet seat and lid, not the entire toilet. You can remove lime and rust stains with a pumice stone, available near the nail polish in any drug store. Replace ugly old medicine cabinets with newer versions. Hang a small wall cabinet over the toilet. Make sure the bathroom fan does not rattle, and replace it if necessary. These small changes can have a significant impact on buyers.

The family room has dark paneling and no windows. What can I do?

The plan for updating the dark paneling look that was so popular in the seventies depends on the anticipated price range for your house. For more expensive homes, you will need to rip out the paneling, repair or replace the drywall underneath, and then paint. For more modest homes, I recommend covering the paneling in a specialty primer and then painting it. Do not try to fill in all the grooves, because that almost never works out well.

Install a window or two, or even expand the space with one of the garden room kits widely available. There are some inexpensive choices on the Internet. If you followed my earlier suggestion about visiting home and garden shows, you probably have brochures from several manufacturers. Additional lighting will also help.

If the family room is in the basement, think about capitalizing on the dark look and turning it into a media room. I am talking about decorative finishes and labeling only, not wiring and electronics. Paint the walls with an acoustic paint or hang dark fabric panels on them. These are simply eight-foot by four-foot lengths of fabric stapled to wooden frames. Put in thick-pile dark carpeting, put a dimmer on the light switch, and spend $100 on a replica old-fashioned popcorn cart. Call the place a media room and you are in business.

What other quick fixes can I do inexpensively?

The choices are limitless. Visit home and garden shows for many ideas. Vendors often have before-and-after pictures to illustrate the value of their products. You can pick up a lot of ideas that way.

Chapter 7

SELLING YOUR HOUSE

- Do I need a real estate agent to sell my home?
- Do I need a real estate license to sell my flips?
- How do I find a good real estate agent?
- How can I make my house more marketable?
- Do I need a marketing plan for the house?
- Can I get my house on MLS without an agent?
- Should I advertise on the Internet?
- What should I do to optimize my presence on the Internet?
- What is the first rule about showing houses?
- How can I show my house to the best advantage?
- People look at a lot of houses. How do I make mine memorable?
- What do I do when the house tour is over?
- If I do not hear from a prospect after a tour, is it okay to call him or her?
- What do I do if a prospective buyer offers me less than my asking price?
- How much earnest money should I request?
- Once I sell my flip property, what are the tax consequences?
- How can I avoid dealer status and higher tax rates?
- Suppose I can honestly be called an investor rather than a dealer. How do I take advantage of the tax-free exchange rules?

Do I need a real estate agent to sell my home?

A good real estate agent is always worth the fee you pay. When my husband and I left Houston in the late 1980s, it was the worst possible time to try to sell a house. The economy was terrible, most of the people in our neighborhood were in bankruptcy, foreclosures were at an all-time high, and there were thousands of houses on the market in our end of Houston. We hired a real estate agent who really made a terrific impression on us. She was energetic, focused, and organized. She told us she had already sold millions of dollars of homes that year, and she had the closing statements to prove it. Her average time-on-market was three months, and her average sales price was 95% of the asking price. We gave her the listing and agreed to pay her a whopping 8% commission.

Three weeks later, we had a signed contract for the full appraised value, which was also our asking price. I did not for one second resent paying that agent an 8% commission. If the house stayed on the market for a year, like those of most of my friends, I would pay far more than 8% in holding costs—interest, taxes, insurance, and utilities.

So, my short answer is, you do not need a real estate agent if all he or she will do is put a sign in your yard, list the property on MLS, and wait for the phone to ring. If you can find a good agent, though, spend the money. You are a flipper, after all, and you must sell that house as quickly as possible.

Do I need a real estate license to sell my flips?

You do not need a real estate license to sell your own properties, or properties owned by a company you own and control.

How do I find a good real estate agent?

First, learn about particular specialties. Most experienced agents specialize in a particular price range, part of town, or type of housing, such as historic homes, starter homes, or retirement communities. It allows them to operate more efficiently. Newer agents tend to work with anyone who wanders through the door. They are less likely to be as knowledgeable as the specialists, but they are also less likely to write you off if they think you foolishly rejected a low but reasonable offer. Decide which attributes you want and choose accordingly.

In addition, some agents specialize in representing sellers, while others specialize in representing buyers. Many do both. The ones who specialize in buyers will usually not have the contacts or experience to effectively market your property.

Next, ask the closing companies for their recommendations. Which agents go to a lot of closings and never seem to have any problems? Compare that list to the specialists you have identified. Schedule about three interviews for the top contenders. Meet at the job site. Have a prepared list of questions, which should include the following.

- How long have you been a real estate agent (or broker)?

- Describe your specialty, and what makes you so successful with that specialty.

- What is your average annual production over the last three years, in dollar volume of houses sold? What was the average price of those houses?

- For the last year, what is the average time on the market for your listings? How does that compare with the community average? For the most part, what percentage of the asking price did sellers receive?

- Describe exactly what you will do to market my property. What makes you so good at capturing callers and turning them into buyers?

- Will you be working this listing, or will it be turned over to another team member? If you use a team concept, can I meet the other members of the team?

- Can you recommend an asking price?

- What changes would you recommend I make in order to maximize my sales price? How much more do you think the house will bring if I follow your suggestions?

- If I hire you, will you provide me with proof of errors and omissions insurance?

- Have you ever been sued by a client, or had a complaint filed against you with the licensing authorities? Will you tell me the details?

At the close of the interviews, you have to evaluate how you feel about the answers you received, and make your choice accordingly.

Million Dollar Producers

Do not be overly impressed with agents who tell you they are "million dollar producers." That means they sold $1 million of real estate last year. With the average commission split among listing brokers, selling brokers, and the agents who actually did the work, someone who sold $1 million of houses made only $12,000 last year. Do you want to hire someone who is proud of making less than they would at McDonald's?

How can I make my house more marketable?

For most flippers, you have already taken the biggest steps to make your property more competitive in the marketplace. This means you fixed everything that was broken, updated everything that was outmoded, freshened up everything that was stale, and cleaned everything that was dirty. Most real estate agents cannot talk their clients into doing those things, so you are way ahead of the market in that regard.

You can gain even more of an advantage by offering incentives not available in other properties. One best seller is the *home warranty program*. You buy insurance from a national company to cover repairs on all major appliances for one year from purchase. Even if all the appliances are brand new and still under manufacturers' warranties, the blanket home warranty still seems more valuable to consumers. For more information about providers and their reputations, check with your state or local Homebuilders Association. The national website at **www.nahb.org** can provide you with phone numbers, or you can call them at 800-368-5242.

Completely installed home security systems, with one year of prepaid monitoring, are another big advantage. Usually the installation is free if you will commit to one year of monitoring, and the monitoring is very inexpensive. In my area, for example, monitoring is less than $20 a month. Why would someone buy one house over another house just because of $240 worth of security monitoring services? I call it "the fooling with it factor." Most people simply do not want to fool with making a choice among security companies and then being present for the installation and the inevitable high-pressure sales to upgrade equipment. They want the system, but they dread going through obtaining the system. If you make that painless, and if you point out they will save money on their insurance because of the monitoring, you will be a hero. They will buy your house. Everyone will be happy.

Another favorite marketing edge is to offer a vacation to the home buyer—a cruise, a long weekend at a resort, or an adventure package. Think about it. Most home buyers feel they have been thoroughly traumatized by the process and deserve a little break. Unfortunately, many will not be able to afford a little break for several years. The lure of a cruise after the closing can give your property the edge you need. Cruise packages can be purchased relatively inexpensively.

An auctioneer taught me this next trick. He said when people want something, they want affirmation from others that they are making the right decision. In addition, when buying a home, they want to know that other people will enjoy coming to the home for activities and entertaining. Using these two concepts, schedule a block party instead of the same old boring open house. Everyone has fun, meets the neighbors, gets the feel of entertaining in their new home, and all the potential buyers affirm each other by saying nice things about the house. Your out-of-pocket expenses will be several hundred dollars, but it is just part of your marketing budget.

Do I need a marketing plan for the house?

In my experience, a marketing plan always works well for two reasons.

1. It forces you to think about how to market the property and how much money you are willing to spend.

2. For most people, a written plan imposes discipline and psychological pressure to do the things on the plan.

My advice to you is to definitely write a marketing plan. There is nothing complicated about it.

> ## Start Selling Before You Buy
>
> Aside from the well-known phrase, "location, location, location," there is another popular saying in the real estate industry. It is: "You make your money when you buy, not when you sell." In other words, buy right, and the profits will follow naturally. To help the process, think about working through a marketing plan on a property before you commit to buying it. If there are any weaknesses, they will become obvious in the marketing plan. You may be able to compensate for them during remodeling, or you may decide to pass on the property and wait for something better.

Can I get my house on MLS without an agent?

You must hire a licensed real estate broker or agent to get your house listed on the local Multiple Listing Service (MLS). Traditionally, the only way to gain access was to sign a full-services listing contract and agree to pay a percentage of the sales price as a commission. Today, so-called *limited services brokers* (LSBs) will list your property on MLS for a flat fee. You can then choose what other brokerage services you desire and are willing to pay for.

One reminder, though. Although billed as "limited" services brokers, almost all LSBs offer the complete range of brokerage services and the traditional full-service brokerage. If your own marketing activities and the MLS exposure do not provide results, you can always add more services from the same real estate broker.

A recent study indicated that sellers without real estate agents sold their homes for more money, but it took longer. You have to evaluate your own numbers in order to make a decision to list or not. What are your monthly holding costs, and what is the commission you will have to pay when the house sells?

Should I advertise on the Internet?

Today, Internet-based information is critical to any marketing campaign. If you do not already have one, get a website. Many companies will reserve a domain name for you and provide hosting, email support for your site, and easy-to-use templates for creating your web page. If you keep your site at five pages or less, you can usually have a presence on the Internet for only $10 a month. More pages—including all you will ever need—will cost you around $15 per month.

What should I do to optimize my presence on the Internet?

Search engines constantly *crawl* the Internet, *bookmarking* and *indexing* websites for future searchers. It can take awhile for a search engine to find you, which is why so many companies sell registration services in order to optimize your presence.

I recommend a different strategy for flippers. Following this strategy will direct people to your home page, where they can click on specific properties as your offerings change from time to time. In addition, searchers will be able to find particular sales pages on your site, even if you frequently change the house spotlighted on that page.

On your home page, include some information that would be useful to anyone searching for a home, particularly in your target demographic market if you have one. Mention certain keywords that searchers are likely to include in their search string if they are candidates for your property. As an example, for starter homes you might include the city, neighborhood, school districts, and the following words:

- home;
- house;
- for sale;

- neighborhood;
- easy commute;
- FSBO;
- for sale by owner;
- good schools; and,
- any other amenities people are likely to search.

The search engines will take note of your home page and the key words on it.

Try to keep the home page exactly the same over time, with no changes. Provide a link to another page, where you will display information about your current property for sale. Use the same keywords on that page, as well.

Additionally, each time you have a different home for sale, update the same information page rather than creating a new one. This is because search engines will remember a particular page address, such as **www.myhomesforsale.com/property**. If you put information about your first flip on a page called "property," and then you put information about your second flip on a page called "nextproperty," then some search engines will still direct people to the "property" page. But that piece of property will not exist anymore because you already sold that house. The interested buyers—who might be interested in buying your second house—will not be able to find you. This is why you want to keep the web page name the same, but simply update the information on that page.

What is the first rule about showing houses?

First and foremost, you should be sensitive to issues regarding your own personal safety. I do not want to frighten you, because millions of real estate agents show houses all the time without incident. They are careful, however, and you should follow their lead.

Think about it. You are making an appointment to meet a complete stranger in an empty house at a date and time of his or her choosing. You do not know how many additional people will be there. Perhaps you did not think to tell anyone where you would be and for how long. Would you let your son, daughter, mother, or sister do this?

Ideally, two of you should be present for all house showings. You should confirm the potential buyer's identity in some manner before meeting him or her at the house—ask for a work number and call him or her at work, for example. Never rely on simply a cell phone number for contact information.

If you will have another person accompany you to the showing, be sure to tell the prospect that information. It may encourage him or her to cancel if he or she was intending to do something sinister. Before leaving for your appointment, tell someone where you are going, how long you expect to be gone, who you are meeting, and the prospect's contact information. Wear flat shoes in case you need to run, and carry something that is legal in your state to protect yourself, such as pepper spray.

When you meet the prospect, make a point of calling someone from your cell phone. Apologize to the prospect for the phone call, but say, "I am required to check in at the beginning of each tour, and again at the end."

If you are careful and sensible, you can avoid becoming a tragic story on the evening news. Again, I cannot stress too much that millions of agents show homes every day, without incident. Some do get robbed, though, and some suffer far worse.

How can I show my house to the best advantage?

Make sure the house is clean and smells fresh and that the lawn is well-manicured and looks maintenance free. We all know that swimming pools, lawns, flower beds, and light-colored carpeting take work to keep them that way. But, we just do not think about it if everything looks perfect. One dandelion in a two-acre lawn can cause a prospect to wonder how many hours a week he or she will spend maintaining the yard.

If the house has any special features, such as energy efficient windows, a lawn sprinkler system, or a fenced yard, make sure to point them out to prospective buyers. Comment about how that feature might be important to your prospect. This is called a *feature/benefit tour*. You point out a feature, and then you describe the benefit.

Compare the following two conversations.

Conversation One
You: "Here is the completely fenced-in back yard."
Prospect thinks:"So? I do not have children or pets."
Prospect says: "That's nice."

Conversation Two
You: "Here is the completely fenced-in back yard. I know you do not have children or pets, but this is a really nice feature because it keeps other people's pets, and their deposits, out of your yard."
Prospect: "That is a really good idea. At my mother's house, the dog next door is always...."

In order to do a successful feature/benefit tour, you must know a little bit about your prospect. Spend some time chatting, just getting to know him or her and any common interests. By doing this, you accomplish three goals.

1. You put your prospect at ease because he or she expects you to start selling right away. When you do not sell, your prospect lets his or her defenses down.

2. You establish common ground, find opportunities to bond, and enhance your credibility.

3. You find out information to use in your feature/benefit tour.

People look at a lot of houses. How do I make mine memorable?

You are right, people do visit a lot of houses when they are shopping. The homes start to run together in their minds. It is a truism in the industry that people will buy the most recent house they remember after they start to tire of the shopping process.

Change that dynamic by coming to the tour with a high-quality digital camera. Take several general photos, but then ask your prospects which particular features they would like photographed. Explain that you will mail them the prints. This not only gives you great insight into the things they find attractive, it also helps memorialize that warm fuzzy feeling they had when they saw those features. They start seeing themselves in the house, enjoying those features. You gain a significant advantage over other properties on the market.

What do I do when the house tour is over?

Ask your prospects how your house compares to others they have seen. Whatever they say, let them talk. Do not argue with them about anything, even if they are completely wrong about something. Thank them for their time and their observations.

If it is obvious the house will not work out for them, tell the prospects that you might have something more suitable in the near future. Ask them about their particular requirements, and then ask if you can contact them if you acquire a home that might work for them. Usually, they will be very candid with you and will invite you to follow up later. This information is very valuable market research for your next flip.

Sometimes, the prospects will have misunderstood something. They will think the house is not right, they cannot afford it, or the school district is different. Pick out what seems to be their most important objection, and correct that misperception if it is possible. For all other objections, wait and write a follow-up card. Thank them for their time, state that you have reflected on their comments, and these are your thoughts on the subject. Then, counter each of their arguments in a very nice, unconfrontational way. In this manner, you have corrected the record, but you have done it in a manner that does not say, "You are wrong and I am right."

The best of all possible worlds is when the prospects give you buying signs. They talk about how to arrange the furniture, colors to paint the walls, and weekend activities. You should be ready for those prospects. Have a contract already printed out, with their names and all information filled in, except for the price. Hand the contract to them and say, "This house seems to be the right one for you. Would you like to take this contract home, think about things, and be prepared to make an offer if you decide you want to go forward?" Never attempt a hard sell to obtain an immediate signature, and never be in the position of having to say, "Can I get a contract prepared in the next day or two and bring it over to you?" You could lose valuable momentum if you have to wait several days to put a contract in their hands.

If I do not hear from a prospect after a tour, is it okay to call him or her?

Not only is this okay, it is highly desirable. When I was new to real estate, I once lost a very important tenant prospect to another building owner. I was crushed because I thought my property was so much better than my prospect's ultimate choice. Several months later I saw that prospect at a charity event. I asked him if he could give me some advice, because I had obviously misread his interest in my property. He said, "Your offices were perfect, but then you never called me back. I figured you rented them to someone else." I was seething—he could have made a simple phone call to find out. But, on the other hand, I could have made a simple phone call to follow up with him.

You are not being pushy when you call a prospect to find out if he or she is still interested in your property. You are being thoughtful and caring and showing respect to people who took the time to visit your house. If you are not used to selling, this is a hard thing to remember. It will pay off for you, though.

What do I do if a prospective buyer offers me less than my asking price?

This will almost certainly happen to you. When faced with an offer that is less than your asking price, you must decide whether to accept it or counter with something else. I generally do not play games with this process. If the buyer's offer is acceptable to me, I accept it. Yes, I might have left some money on the table, but my time is too valuable to waste a month haggling. In addition, you run the risk of losing your buyer during that time. He or she might decide the house is too expensive, or he or she might continue shopping and find something he or she likes better.

If you decide to negotiate, try to find out whether or not the prospective buyers have miscalculated the value of your house or if they are just bargain hunters. Your approach will be different for each one.

A person who cannot afford your house might be a prospect for your next flip. Be polite, but find out what he or she wants, and what a realistic price range would be. If his or her goals are unrealistic, he or she might be a tenant prospect if you sell your house to an investor. Think about that route before burning any bridges.

People who miscalculate the value of your home and make a lowball offer can usually be persuaded otherwise. Indicate your willingness to be educated regarding their perception of the marketplace. Ask for details regarding other home sales they think are comparable or any evidence on which they base their opinion of value. Once you know that, you can usually demonstrate that your home is worth more than they thought.

The bargain shoppers fall into two camps—those who love the thrill of negotiations, and those who love the bragging rights of a cheap price. Both want you to put up a good fight and then lose gracefully but reluctantly and with mutterings about how you are not making any money. For such people, you must lower your price in small increments, but ask for something else in return. As an example, you could say, "I would be willing to reduce the price by $5,000, but only if we schedule closing within fourteen days instead of the typical thirty days."

How much earnest money should I request?

First, please revisit the earnest money questions in Chapter 3 on buying a property to flip. All the same principles apply, but you are now on the opposite side of the fence.

Request an amount large enough to show you the buyer has financial resources. You do not want to waste your time on someone with little or no cash and high hopes of finding financing.

In addition, think about the hostage value of the earnest money. A small amount could be pocket change—a buyer might abandon the earnest money and elect to buy something else that seems more desirable or even less expensive. One of my client/sellers once accepted $500 earnest money on a $198,000 home. Thirty days later, on the day before closing, the buyer advised that she would not proceed to purchase. She had found another house for only $187,900 and was all too happy to breach her purchase contract with my client and lose her $500.

Once I sell my flip property, what are the tax consequences?

Right now, let us discuss all flips except the homeowner flip. We will cover that in another question.

First, you must decide if you are truly in the business of flipping houses, or if you are an investor who does this sporadically. The IRS calls you a *dealer* if you hold property primarily for sale to customers in the ordinary course of business. You are an *investor* if you are a passive owner of real estate for future increase in value.

Investors receive the advantage of much lower long-term capital gains tax rates, and may be eligible for tax-deferred sales called *1031 exchanges*. Dealers pay taxes at their normal tax bracket percentage for ordinary income, and they must pay the self-employment tax that is equivalent to Social Security and Medicare withholding.

At the time this book was written, the highest tax rates for each category were as follows:

Long-term capital gains	15%
Ordinary income	35%
Self-employment income	15.8%

How can I avoid dealer status and higher tax rates?

I wish there was a simple answer to this question, but there is not. Life would be terrific if the IRS had set concrete rules and guidelines. In reality, though, it does have one simple rule: dealers hold property for resale to customers in the ordinary course of business. All flippers are dealers. The arguments and lawsuits arise over what is meant by the words "in the ordinary course of business."

Over the course of many years and many lawsuits between taxpayers and the IRS, we are left with some guidelines on this question. Primarily it is a matter of considering several factors, and then analyzing if those factors point toward investor or dealer. It is only the most rare occasions when one factor, all by itself, will result in someone being a dealer.

The factors are:

- the number and frequency of sales (there is no magic number that pushes you over into dealer status);

- the extent of improvements (massive improvements usually indicate a dealer);

- the sales efforts (A "for sale" sign in the yard indicates an investor; a large advertising campaign indicates a dealer. You probably fall in the middle somewhere.);

- the purpose for acquiring, holding, and selling the property (If you acquired the property with the intention of reselling it fairly quickly in order to make a profit, you are a dealer. That one catches most flippers.);

- the manner in which the property was acquired (generally, if you inherit property or receive it by gift, you are more likely to be classified as an investor);

- the holding period (The longer you hold property before resale, the less likely it is that you are an investor. There are no time limit rules here. Waiting one year and one day to sell property does not guarantee your status as an investor, contrary to advice in some other books.);

- the percentage of income from real estate activities (the higher the percentage, the more likely you are a dealer);

- the use of proceeds (using the money to buy another house— more inventory—tends to indicate a dealer); and,

- how you present yourself to the community (if you call yourself a flipper and actively solicit flip opportunities from others, you are probably a dealer).

Suppose I can honestly be called an investor rather than a dealer. How do I take advantage of the tax-free exchange rules?

"Tax-free" is a little misleading because it is really "tax-deferred." You pay no income tax at the time of sale, but you do pay it eventually. The process is called a *1031 exchange*. As long as you keep selling properties and quickly buying more, meeting all the requirements of section 1031 of the Internal Revenue Code, you can keep delaying your taxes.

In a nutshell, this is how it works. First you sell the first property. The IRS calls this the *relinquished property*. All the sale proceeds must be kept in escrow by someone called a *qualified intermediary*.

Usually, this is a closing attorney or escrow company. You have 45 days from the sale of the first property to *identify* the new piece of real estate you want to buy. The IRS calls the new property the *replacement property*. You identify the property in a writing you give to your qualified intermediary.

You can pick up to three properties to identify, but you must buy one of those properties within 180 days of the sale of the first property. If you do it exactly right, you do not pay any taxes this year on the sale of the first property.

The technical details regarding other requirements can get pretty complicated. For more information, you should read IRS Publication 544, "Sales and Other Dispositions of Assets," and Form 8824, "Like-Kind Exchanges," available at **www.irs.gov**. If you do anything wrong in this process, you will have to pay taxes in the year of the sale. This is not an area for do-it-yourself work. Hire a tax professional to assist you.

Chapter 8

PLAN B

- What are my options if I break my budget with repairs and cannot afford to spend any more money?
- If I get into financial trouble, can I just give the house to the bank and cut my losses?
- What should I tell my lender if it looks like the house will not sell as quickly as I thought?
- Flippers on television say it is easier to sell a house if they hold the financing. How does that work?
- What documents will I need to fill out if I agree to hold the financing for a house I sell?
- Can I rent out my house until I find a buyer?
- How do I find good tenants?
- What Fair Housing laws do I need to know before renting my house?
- Are there any exemptions to the Fair Housing laws?
- Can I perform a background check on potential tenants?
- What paperwork will I need for a rental house?
- Do I need to know any specific landlord/tenant laws?
- Which lease clauses are going to be especially important to me?
- How much rent should I charge?
- How much security deposit should I collect?
- Should I give my tenant an option to buy the property?
- Should I hire a professional management company?
- How much will it cost to hire a management company?
- How do I choose a good management company?
- If I manage my rental house myself, what issues might arise that are important to know about ahead of time?
- What if my tenant does not pay the rent?
- How do I prevent a tenant from damaging my property?
- What are my rights if my tenant files for Chapter 13 bankruptcy?

What are my options if I break my budget with repairs and cannot afford to spend any more money?

Believe it or not, running out of repair money is not the disaster you might fear. Certainly, you should be very careful in how you prepare your budgets and conserve money—that goes without saying. Sometimes, though, you will run into surprises that you just could not have anticipated. If you find yourself in such a situation, there are at least four different routes you can take.

The first route—which is the most desirable one—is to discuss the change in events with your lender. Be sure you do it as soon as it looks like you might have problems, rather than waiting until you have put yourself even deeper in debt. Bankers are generally very organized people who like to plan their affairs. At the same time, they also know that nothing is ever a guaranteed sure thing and that there are risks involved in every project. The trick is to let your lender know there has been a surprise, and then give him or her enough time to digest the information, consider all his or her alternatives, and work with you to come up with a plan to work through the problem. None of us make our best decisions under extreme pressure at the last minute. If you avoid talking to your banker and put off the conversation until you have completely run out of money, owe money to subcontractors, and cannot make your next interest payment to the bank, then you might not be happy with the final solution your lender comes up with.

By talking about your potential financial problems at the very first sign of trouble, this demonstrates to your lender that you are a prudent business person and someone likely to successfully overcome temporary setbacks. Estimate the additional money and time you think will be necessary to complete the job. Be realistic and even a bit conservative in your estimate. This is no time to be wildly optimistic and then have to go back to your lender again in a few months for even more money. Request the additional loan money upfront to meet your needs. If necessary, offer to drop the asking price when you are ready to sell so the house will sell more quickly. This tells your lender that you are willing to personally take a smaller profit, or even just break even, if the lender will assume more risk by loaning you more money.

The second route you might be able to take is to find a partner who can inject some cash into the project. This rarely works out for people, so do not put this strategy high on your list. A partner who comes in at the last minute to save your project when you break the budget usually wants all of the profit when the house ultimately sells. Even on those terms, it is difficult to find an investor on short notice when you are also dealing with the emotional and economic pressures of running out of money. If you do find someone, you will spend several more weeks or months completing the project and working for free. There is no pot of gold at the end of the rainbow if you have to give away all of your potential profits just to prevent a foreclosure. You would probably be better off selling your home to another flipper, taking your losses, and getting on with life.

The third route you can take to get out of your predicament is to sell the house to another flipper. While they will ultimately make the profit you intended to earn yourself, you will have escaped from the project, will not have lost any money, and can spend your time on another project that has a greater potential of turning a profit for you. In business, it is important to know when to take your losses.

The fourth strategy involves believing in yourself, and requires good salesmanship and the ability to put a positive spin on anything. Here is how it works.

Let us assume that your first business plan called for $35,000 worth of repairs that would result in a home that was move-in ready and could sell for a $50,000 profit. After spending about $15,000 on unforeseen structural problems related to an old roof leak and a lot of rotten wood, you see that you cannot complete the house according to your original plan. Instead, you can spend your remaining $20,000 on life, safety, and comfort items, such as heating and air conditioning, working electricity and plumbing, and doors and windows that can be secured. Next, make sure there is at least one working bathroom, a sink and working plumbing in the kitchen, and the necessary electrical outlets for a stove and a refrigerator. In most cities, these are the minimum elements necessary to obtain a certificate of occupancy (C/O). If you have any money left, fix up the entryway and the landscaping to make a good first impression.

With your certificate of occupancy, someone can now legally live in the property while he or she completes the other repairs and remodeling. Once you obtain a certificate of occupancy, you will be able to sell the house, even though it will bring in less amount of money. Likely candidates include homebuyers on limited budgets but who are handy and can do their own finishing work. This target market is small, but it is very focused. Few houses on the market will meet their needs, but your house can be one of the few that would be desirable and attainable for these buyers.

In the same vein, do not discount the idea of putting a positive spin on your problem and still making a large profit. Once you discover and repair all the surprises, you now have a house with no surprises for the next owner. This can be worth a lot to potential buyers who have a desire to remodel and customize their perfect home but are not do-it-yourselfers. These people do not want to buy a house stamped with your idea of kitchen layout, plumbing fixtures, paint color, and wallpaper patterns. They do not want to spend time and money ripping out everything you did, just so they can do it all over again their way. You should paint all the walls white, leave clean but unfinished floors, and install very plain and inexpensive light fixtures. Then obtain a very detailed inspection report that you can show it to prospective purchasers.

Once you do this, you can market your home as being in "perfect condition, but ready to re-decorate and customize." Sell it as is, or offer to customize the home according to the buyer's specifications. Establish a budget for meeting the specifications, require the buyer to pay for all labor and materials, obtain a fairly large earnest money check, and set a closing date a few days after completion of all work. You can potentially still make your original profit, and perhaps even more. Custom homes always cost more per square foot than what are called spec homes, or a home that is completed by a builder with standardized finishes and details, and then sold to someone else.

The trick to overcoming possibly disastrous surprises is to plan for their possibility in advance. If you anticipate problems and allow for the possibility they might happen, you will not be shocked into paralysis if they do come about. People who have contingency plans prepared ahead of time generally have very creative solutions and good plans. When you are in the middle of a crisis, you will not have the time or the patience to start thinking of legitimate solutions. Follow your predetermined plans, stay calm, and everything will usually work out fine.

If I get into financial trouble, can I just give the house to the bank and cut my losses?

Many people think that if they get into financial trouble on a project, they can give their lender the mortgaged property, wash their hands of the whole mess, and simply walk away with only the loss of their earnest money and time. Unfortunately, this is not the way things work. The mechanism of giving property to a lender, without the trauma of a foreclosure, is called a *deed in lieu of foreclosure*. Most insiders simply refer to it as a deed in lieu.

The first problem with a deed in lieu is that lenders do not like them, especially if you have been remodeling or making repairs to the property. When a lender gets a deed in lieu, the lender has to take the property subject to all other liens and claims on it, which includes those that could be made by your subcontractors and suppliers. No lender wants to get stuck with additional liens or claims on a piece of property.

The second problem with a deed in lieu is that it does not necessarily wipe out your loan. The rules vary from state to state, and also according to your negotiations with your lender. You could easily suffer the loss of the real estate and still owe a very large sum of money to the bank. The reason for this is because the lender will give you credit for less than the fair market value of the house in its current condition. Half-finished houses have fairly depressed values, which is why successful flippers are able to make a profit on the pieces of property. The lender gives a credit less than the fair market value, so it has a cushion in case it estimated the value incorrectly, as well as to cover itself for holding costs until it can sell to someone else. The same analysis goes into calculating a bid price for a foreclosure. As a result, giving the house back to the bank, or letting it go to foreclosure, will usually not solve any problems and will probably cause more.

In very rare circumstances, you may be able to negotiate what is called a non-recourse note. This means that the lender agrees to loan you money secured by real estate, but also agrees to look only to the real estate for recovery of its loan in case you default. In other words, the lender agrees in advance that it will not sue the borrower after a default, but simply foreclose on the real estate. Successfully negotiating non-recourse notes are almost always to long-term financing on large income-producing properties like apartments, office buildings, and shopping centers. Sometimes, so called hard money lenders will loan you 50% of the value of real estate on a non-recourse basis and at high interest rates. It would be extremely difficult to find a flip that qualifies. You should not waste your time going from lender to lender to lender, hunting for the elusive non-recourse financing for your house flip.

What should I tell my lender if it looks like the house will not sell as quickly as I thought?

As soon as you see problems, you should talk to your lender. He or she might tell you that the entire market is soft, meaning that sales are slow to occur. Your lender will be sympathetic because everyone is in the same boat. It also means your lender probably has other borrowers with the same sales problems. Your lender will probably not want to make waves, declare defaults, and start a massive string of foreclosures. Instead, your lender will probably be motivated to work with you and renew your note for an additional three to six months. If you will not be able to make the interest payments during the prolonged period, discuss that, as well. Tell your lender you want a single pay renewal, with all principal and accrued interest due at maturity instead of paying interest every month.

On the other hand, your lender might tell you that home sales are strong, and he or she does not understand why you cannot sell your property. This is actually better news for you because it means you can change your marketing or pricing and sell your house. Discuss alternatives with the banker and come to an agreement regarding a plan. With a realistic plan and your promise to follow the plan, most lenders will renew the note to give you additional time to sell your property instead of foreclosing on it right away.

Flippers on television say it is easier to sell a house if they hold the financing. How does that work?

Many people can afford a down payment and monthly mortgage payments but do not qualify for traditional home loans. Perhaps they had a recent problem that destroyed their credit rating but not their ability to pay bills on time. Often, massive medical bills, credit card problems, or business reversals push people into bankruptcy. They emerge with a clean slate but a terrible credit score. While they might still be able to borrow money somewhere, they will have to pay much higher interest rates on the money they borrow. Many such people are good credit risks. They have few choices in homes, because they must buy a home that offers seller financing. If you have such a home for sale, you will have little competition on the market.

There are two methods of selling a home and holding the financing. Both require the cooperation and approval of your lender. You probably borrowed money on a short-term basis to acquire the house and then flip it fairly quickly. Things are now different. You and your lender will need to agree on a longer term for your loan with regular monthly payments. Because almost all mortgages contain a due on sale clause, which makes the loan due in full if the property is sold, you will need your lender to agree to waive that clause.

The first financing method is a traditional sale, in which you give the buyer a deed and he or she takes the property subject to your lender's first mortgage. The buyer also gives you a mortgage, which wraps around the first mortgage. The buyer makes payments to you, and then you make payments to your lender.

You need to know, however, that there are severe tax consequences if you do not structure this exactly type of financing exactly right. In a nutshell, if the buyer makes payments directly to your lender, or does anything to make sure their payments to you will result in payments to your lender, you could owe huge taxes but without the cash to pay them. This is because the IRS will take the position that you made all your profit in the year of the sale, even though your money will come in over several years. With normal seller financing, the seller splits each mortgage payment into two parts—a refund of his investment and a profit on his investment. Only the profit portion of each payment is taxable during that year. A seller who spends $120,000 to buy and fix up a house, and then sells it for $180,000 and holds the financing, might have only a few hundred dollars of taxable profit in the first year. A seller who does a wrap around mortgage, and who does not follow the IRS rules exactly, will have $60,000 of taxable profit in the first year. Please consult a tax professional for advice on how to avoid this consequence with proper planning.

The second popular method of seller financing for flippers is the contract for deed, also called a bond for title and sometimes a land sale contract. In this arrangement, the buyer does not receive a deed to the property until they have made all payments in full. It is a good arrangement for the seller, because if the buyer defaults, the seller can usually evict the buyer immediately. There is no lengthy foreclosure process, and even a last-minute bankruptcy will generally not save the purchaser and allow him or her to remain in the property. These are the same factors that make this very risky for buyers. As a result, usually only the most desperate buyers, or the most unsophisticated ones, will agree to such an arrangement. The process is strongly disfavored by many states and courts because of the high risk that a buyer might forfeit substantial equity as a result of a minor default. For that reason, some states have consumer protection laws that heavily regulate such relationships and provide safety nets for defaulting buyers. Be sure to check Appendix E at the back of this book, call your state's real estate department or consumer affairs office, and find out the law in your jurisdiction.

What documents will I need to fill out if I agree to hold the financing for a house I sell?

Please consult with a local attorney to answer this question. All states are different. At the very least, traditional financing will require a promissory note and a mortgage or a deed of trust, depending on your state. You might want to include a security agreement and a UCC-1, to cover anything on the property that might possibly be classified as personal property instead of real property, such as a swing set or portable storage building.

Obtain a copy of the documents for your own home, or that of a friend or relative, to use as a sample. Do not use the mortgage on your flip property because that is classified as a commercial loan. The bank uses different forms and has different legal requirements for commercial loans than for home loans. The reason you want to look at some bank forms is because they are usually very strongly written in favor of the lender. Forms you obtain from a book, or off the Internet, or even from an attorney, might be less protective of your interests. Read everything, and compare the bank's documents to the ones you propose to use. Are there any clauses you should add? Is there anything you do not understand? Make sure you understand what you are signing, and are comfortable with the final agreement.

You will also need something in writing from your lender waiving the due on sale clause. You must have this in writing. It is not a matter of whether or not to trust your loan officer. If he or she transfers, receives a promotion, changes employers, or retires, someone else will be in charge of your loan. In many circumstances, the bank is not bound by anything that is not in writing and part of their books and records. In other words, if you and your original loan officer both swear under oath that you can sell the house without paying off the loan, the bank can still say, "We don't care, it doesn't bind us." They can call your note, demand payment in full, and proceed to foreclosure if you do not pay up.

To be on the safe side, I would also obtain something in writing from an accountant or other tax professional that your documents meet IRS requirements so you do not have large taxable income in the year of the sale. If there is a problem that is discovered later on, that is not the time to start finger-pointing about who said what. A piece of paper, asking for a signature, tends to cause people to pay more attention and give more careful answers.

If you want to go the route of a contract for deed, go to the place were deeds are recorded in your jurisdiction. Often, people record contracts for deed in the real estate records. Obtain copies of several. Read them and make sure you understand the various clauses. Then hire an attorney to draft something for you, and compare the final product to the forms you copied. See if you need any changes in the finished product. As a practical consideration, I usually do not like to give people copies of forms I find. I think it structures their thinking, and prevents them from being creative and coming up with independent solutions. After the fact, I use my forms as a checklist, to make sure all the bases are covered.

Can I rent out my house until I find a buyer?

Most flippers who are unable to sell quickly will put tenants in their properties. It has the benefit of providing monthly income to help pay your own holding costs—interest, taxes, and insurance. The tenant pays the utility bills. It keeps down your insurance costs because insurance for vacant houses is often much higher than for occupied homes. In addition, some theft and vandalism losses are often not covered at all if the property is vacant for some period of time.

Your lender will be much more willing to renew your note if you have a tenant in place. It shows that you have taken steps to minimize your losses, and acted in a businesslike manner.

On the negative side, tenants can damage your property, making it harder to sell without spending more money for repairs. At the very least, the most careful tenant in the world will cause some wear and tear, meaning the house will no longer be move-in perfect for a new owner. On the other hand, very few buyers expect perfect homes, so that should not affect your sale price.

Another word of caution about tenants. An acquaintance of mine once rented a large home in a very desirable part of town. He lived there for several years, and then the owner decided to sell. My friend was paying rent substantially lower than similar properties in the market. Plus, he was nested in to the house and comfortable. He did not want to move, but he also could not afford to pay the asking price. He did graciously offer to show the house to prospective buyers, so the owner would not have to drop everything each time someone called. On the morning of each showing, he did three things. In the summer, he turned off the air conditioning and in the winter he turned off the heat. Next, he brought an overflowing cat litter box into the house, rather than its normal spot in a shed. Finally, he flipped a few circuit breakers so that, as he entered rooms and tried to turn on the lights, he could complain about the wiring and then correct the situation by flipping the circuit breaker back into the on position. The poor owner received no offers. After a year, she sold the house to the tenant at a deep discount. Don't let this happen to you!

This story also points out the biggest problem with tenants—they move into the house because they want to live in the house. No one wants to sign a lease with a clause saying the landlord can kick them out if he or she sells the house. Normal landlords can pass that off as boilerplate, and say it is just in case but not likely to happen. You will be different, because you will be actively trying to sell the property, from the start. As a result, you might have problems attracting tenants.

One solution is to find a tenant, put them in place with a standard one-year lease, and then sell your house as a piece of income-producing property to an investor. This may or may not be a good strategy. Depending on where the house is located, an investor might pay more or less money than a homeowner. Be sure to research this issue before choosing this route. Also, most investors base their buying decisions on something called the NOI—Net Operating Income—from a property. In other words, what is the cash flow after receiving all the rent each year and then paying all expenses except mortgage payments? Obviously, the higher the rent, the larger the NOI and the more an investor will be willing to pay. You cannot put a tenant in the house at a discounted rent and then expect to sell the property based on what the rent should be with a different landlord.

How do I find good tenants?

You will obtain the largest number of potential tenants by placing ads in the local newspaper, putting a "For Rent" sign in the yard, and registering with various Internet services such as **www.rentals.com** and **www.rentalhouses.com**. I recommend providing your cell phone number rather than a home or work number. That way, you will be sure to receive all calls, and no one will accidentally erase your messages or neglect to take a written message.

You will obtain the best and most qualified tenants by personal outreach and referrals. Ask neighbors if they know anyone who would like to rent your house. Neighbors, especially homeowners, will want to make sure your tenant is someone who will take care of the property and keep the neighborhood looking nice. Visit nearby apartments, if possible. Many apartment dwellers would love to move into a home in the same general area and school zone. Contact local religious leaders, and ask if you can put an announcement in the weekly newsletter or on a bulletin board, or if they will refer community members to you. Keep track of foreclosure notices, especially those on homes in the same general area. An owner facing foreclosure is not necessarily a poor credit risk, and might make an excellent tenant.

Offering to pay a referral fee is not always a good idea because in many states, paying a referral fee for rentals is illegal unless the other person has a real estate license. For real estate agents, the typical referral fee is one month's rent.

What Fair Housing laws do I need to know before renting my house?

There are two sources of Fair Housing laws, which prohibit a wide variety of discriminatory practices. The federal laws are an absolute minimum that apply in all fifty states. Some states have greater protections for residents within their borders. You can find information by going to the website of the U.S. Department of Housing and Urban Development (HUD) at **www.hud.gov/offices/fheo/index.cfm**. Appendix E to this book also contains the websites for local HUD offices in your states, and your local attorney general's office of consumer affairs.

As a general matter, the federal laws prohibit discrimination if it is based on one of the so-called suspect classifications. They include:

- race;

- alienage (not a citizen);

- color;

- sex;

- religion;

- age;

- national origin;

- marital status;

- disability;

- family status (families with children under 19); and,

- some states include protections based on sexual orientation and other factors.

There are three common types of illegal discrimination. The first is explicit discrimination, which means refusing to do something based on the presence of one of the suspect classifications. This would be if you refused to rent to Latinos, for example, or families with young children. The second type is called disparate impact discrimination. It arises when you do something that does not seem discriminatory on its face, but which has a greater adverse impact on some groups than on other groups. As an example, a landlord might refuse to rent to victims of domestic violence in order to minimize the risk of future violence in the rental property. Since most victims of domestic violence are women, this policy would have a greater impact on women than on men. It would be disparate impact—different impact—discrimination. The third type is called refusal to make reasonable accommodations. It occurs when someone with a disability asks you to make a reasonable adjustment for his or her benefit, and you refuse. For more examples, and guidelines, check out the U.S. Department of Justice website pages at **www.ada.gov**.

Are there any exemptions to the Fair Housing laws?

Federal Fair Housing laws do not apply to certain groups of people, but your state laws might not contain those exemptions. In order to find out your state laws, contact the local office of the U.S. Department of Housing and Urban Development, or your state's consumer affairs section of the attorney general's office. This information is in Appendix E.

Under the federal rules, the following are subject to the fair housing laws:

- real estate licensees;

- individual owners of single family rental/sale houses, but only if:

    1. they use a real estate broker for the property; and/or,
    2. they use discriminatory advertising;

- individual owners of single family rental/sale houses if they own more than three or if they sell more than one every two years (even if they do not use a broker and do not use discriminatory advertising);

- everyone else (corporations, partnerships, etc.) that owns single family homes for rental or sale;

- all owners of multi-family homes of five or more units; and,

- all owners of multi-family homes of four or less units if the owner does not live in one of them.

Can I perform a background check on potential tenants?

Not only can you do a background check, you should do so. You can refuse to rent to someone because of bad credit or a criminal background, as long as you have firm rules and do not apply them on a case-by-case basis. This is because a disorganized approach to which tenants you accept, and which tenants you turn down, could expose you to claims of illegal discrimination.

There are many commercial services that provide background check services for you, or that make them available online. Check with other landlords or property management firms in your town for guidance regarding which resources they find most useful. Some online resources include **http://consumer-guide.to/Background.Checks** and **www.onsite.com**. Also, do not overlook your state's registries for sex offenders.

What paperwork will I need for a rental house?

Before beginning the search for a tenant, make sure you have a lease form you are willing to sign immediately. Many a deal has been lost because one side or the other said, "Can I get back to you with a contract after I talk to my lawyer?" Before your lawyer even returns your phone call, your tenant prospect will have found somewhere else to live.

In addition, you will need a rental application that provides some standard background information such as current employer and length of employment, current residence address and length of time at that address, all prior addresses for the last five years, and contact information for the current landlord and permission to contact him or her as a reference. Of course, you want to be very careful about checking a current landlord for information about there tenant—that landlord might come down on their rent, or offer other incentives, if they know their tenant is shopping for something different. You should ask how many people will be living in the house, but you are not allowed to ask about the ages of the people. Most jurisdictions let you limit residents to no more than two per bedroom without running afoul of any antidiscrimination laws.

You should have a form giving you permission to run a background check, including obtaining a credit report and score. There should be a space for the prospective tenant to put his or her social security number. Make sure you keep those applications in a safe place, and do not discard them in the trash unless they have been shredded. Otherwise, you could contribute to identify theft.

Depending on your local laws, you may have an obligation to determine that your tenant is a legal resident of the United States. It is a good idea to do this, even if not required under the law. The most common forms of proof include:

- Official birth certificate issued by a U.S. state, jurisdiction, or territory (Puerto Rico, U.S. Virgin Islands, Northern Mariana Islands, American Samoa, Swain's Island, Guam);

- U.S. Government-issued certified birth certificate;

- U.S. Certificate of Birth Abroad (DS-1350 or FS-545);

- Report of Birth Abroad of a Citizen of the U.S. (FS-240);

- Valid or expired U.S. passport;

- Certificate of Citizenship (N560 or N561);

- Certificate of Naturalization (N550, N570 or N578);

- Unexpired U.S. Active Duty/Retiree/Reservist Military ID Card (DOD DD-2);

- U.S. Citizen Identification Card (I-197, I-179);

- INS I-551 Permanent Resident Alien Card (the so-called green card);

- Foreign passport stamped by the U.S. Government indicating that the holder has been Processed for I-551;

- Permanent Resident Re-entry Permit (I-327);

- Temporary I-551 stamp on Form I-94, Arrival/Departure Record, with photograph of applicant;;

- U.S. Department of Receptions and Placement Program Assurance Form (Refugee) and I-94 stamped refugee; and,

- Form I-94 Record of Arrival and Departure stamped Asylee, Parolee or Parole, refugee, asylum, HP (humanitarian parolee), or PIP (public interest parolee).

Do I need to know any specific landlord/tenant laws?

Many states have specialized landlord/tenant statutes for residential properties. You should check with your state's Department of Real Estate or Real Estate Commission for more information, or the consumer affairs office of the state attorney general's office. Website information for each state is provided in Appendix E.

If present, such laws usually limit the amount of security deposits, impose a minimum standard of living quality for the residence, outlaw certain one-sided clauses in leases, require landlords to provide a few days' notice before entering the lease premises, and allow a relatively short eviction process during which the tenant must pay its rent to the court even if contesting the eviction on some legally-allowed grounds. There are usually deadlines for returning security deposits. Landlords can be liable for damages and legal fees for very technical violations of the law that would not seem to have caused any harm. For that reason, it is important to find out the requirements in your particular state.

Even without such specialized laws, any landlord should be familiar with the general landlord/tenant law for his or her state. Refer to Appendix E for more specific information on your state. In addition, many local governments impose a rental tax on residential properties located within their jurisdiction. Find out if there are any such taxes, and the amounts.

Which lease clauses are going to be especially important to me?

Aside from the possible ability to sell the house and cancel the lease, there are other clauses that should be especially important to you. Most of them deal with maintaining the condition of the unit.

First and foremost, you should not allow any pets. It sounds heartless and may cost you some tenant prospects. On the other hand, even a small dog or cat can cause thousands of dollars of damage due to clawing walls, floors, and wood trim. Pet hair in the HVAC system can result in breakdowns. Urine odors will discourage buyers, but urine itself can damage carpet, padding, sub-flooring, baseboards, and drywall. The territorial markings of a male cat will never come out of the surfaces marked. Even mice and hamsters can escape to spaces between walls and floors, where they can breed or die and cause horrific odors. They can also easily destroy electrical and phone wiring. A small, leaking aquarium can destroy your flooring. A cat litter box can cause unpleasant smells when you are trying to show the house. Even outdoor pets can damage the landscaping, and will almost certainly be brought into the house during very bad weather.

In the same vein, do not allow smoking in the house. Ask that all cigarette debris be placed in containers, rather than thrown on the ground at the back door, for example.

Next, you should have a clause requiring a certain level of cleanliness. Many of my college students complain that their leases require the premises be kept clean, dishes washed at least daily, and garbage taken out every other day. They must have a clear path of travel into each of the rooms and to the exits. My students say, in essence, that they should be allowed to live in squalor if they choose. When I point out that the issue is one of vermin, disease, and safety, they understand and concede that the clauses are reasonable. You should remember that you will be showing this house to prospective purchasers. You do not want it to look like a pigsty.

You should reserve to yourself responsibility for pest control and lawn care. That way, you make sure it is done properly each time. It also gives you a reason to regularly visit the house and check that all is well.

Make the tenant responsible for notifying you immediately regarding any problems and the need for any repairs. In addition, inspect the property once a month. My oldest stepdaughter once suffered thousands of dollars of damage in a rental house because an antique claw-foot bathtub leaked. Rather than report the problem, the tenants decided it was minor and decided not to tell my stepdaughter because they did not want to bother her. The tenants dealt with the problem by covering up the ugly place on the floor with a very large bathmat. When they moved out, my stepdaughter discovered the floor was rotted nearly through and the tub in danger of falling to the first story of the house.

How much rent should I charge?

The rent you charge must be based on market rents for similar properties. If you feel you need a competitive edge in order to attract a tenant quickly, do not offer discounted rent. There are two reasons for this. Almost any investor who wants to buy your house and keep the tenants in place will base his or her purchase price on the rent you actually charge, not on what you should charge if you charged market rates. Second, if your strategy changes and you decide to keep the house as an investment, you will have a hard time raising the rent to market rates when the lease expires. As an example, suppose the market for similar properties is $1,200 per month. You charge only $1,000, thinking this is a short-term relationship. Your plans change, and at the end of the first year the tenant asks to renew the lease. By that time, market rents are at $1,300 per month, but your tenant has been paying only $1,000 per month. You will almost never be able to raise their rent by $300 per month. You will either lose the tenant, or you will have to raise the rent by only $100 a month.

Instead of discounting rent, offer some other incentive. The typical incentive is the first month's rent free. In the example above, if market rents are at $1,200, but you agree to only $1,000, your tenant saves $2,400 over the course of a year. If you give the first month free, the tenant saves only $1,200 but it all occurs at move-in, when they most need to save money.

Rent control issues are not widespread and are beyond the scope of this book. If you operate in an environment with such restrictions, be sure to obtain local advice so you do not violate the law.

How much security deposit should I collect?

You should collect at least one month's rent as a security deposit. In many states, an amount equal to one month's rent is the most security deposit you can charge. Please re-read the question about landlord/tenant law for guidance. I generally do not like to waive the security deposit. I tell my tenant prospects that it is not a reflection of their economic stability, it is just good business.

If the deposit seems to be a deal breaker, offer to let the tenant pay it in installments over three months instead of all at once. This will usually solve the problem of a tenant with insufficient cash to pay the first month's rent, security deposit, utility deposits, and moving expenses, all at once. On the few occasions when I do waive a security deposit, I always have a trip wire clause in my lease. It says that the first time the tenant is even one day late with the rent, I have the right to demand a security deposit and declare a default if the tenant does not pay the deposit within ten days.

Should I give my tenant an option to buy the property?

It is usually not a good idea to give your tenant an option to buy the property unless you plan to be a long-term landlord. Remember, you originally planned to flip that house. The only reason you even have a tenant is because something did not work out the way you planned. Technically, the presence of a tenant is an obstacle to selling the property to someone who wants to live there. While you can potentially sell to an investor, if the tenant has a contract with a purchase option, no investor is going to be interested except at a very deep discount.

On the other hand, if you and your lender are reconciled to being landlords for a year or more, then a lease option might be a good idea. The strategy has a name and is called the grow your own buyer plan. If the person can afford it, the best prospect to buy a house is almost always going to be the person living in it as a tenant. Just make sure you do not have another flipper for a tenant. That person will tie up your property with his or her purchase option, but only exercise the option if they can make a profit on a quick resale.

Should I hire a professional management company?

A professional management company is usually a good idea if the dollars work out right and if the management company is reputable. Professional management companies generally have the contacts and expertise to quickly find tenants and manage your property to maintain its value. The company will be much more familiar with legal requirements than you, have all the right forms, and have the software to do things more efficiently. They are less likely to become personally involved with a tenant, and therefore better able to be strict about timely rent payment and other requirements. A good management company will keep your rents at market rates, and advise you when you should raise the rent.

The problem you have as a flipper is that you are probably a project-driven person. You like to throw yourself into something, get it done, and go on to something else. You are usually not the type of person who likes to deal with the routine and never-ending chores necessary to properly manage a rental property. As a result, most of the time these things just do not get done. It is better that you should recognize this about yourself, and hire someone else to handle the management.

How much will it cost to hire a management company?

Property managers usually charge a percentage of the rent they collect, generally in the range of 8% to 10%. Some charge extra for customized reports, inspections, and evictions. Many keep all tenant-paid fees for the rental application, late charges, and check overdraft fees. Be aware that late fee income is a significant source of revenue for many companies. While if you were managing the property, you might call a tenant on the 5th of the month to remind him or her that there will be a late charge if no payment is received, a management company might not do that because they want to collect the late fee. The problem is, many tenants realize that being six days late is all the same as being 29 days late, because the late fee is the same. As a result, when they pass the date when a late fee is due, they often wait even longer to pay their rent.

You will be responsible for paying all repair expenses. Some management contracts give the company the right to do minor repairs themselves, or hire outside people, without your prior approval. Ask about the dollar limits for these situations. Also ask about the labor rates and materials markups, and if the management company or a related company does the repairs.

Be sure to ask about reimbursements for travel, telephone calls, copies, and the like. These can be important profit centers for some management companies. You might find yourself being billed an additional $20 to $30 a month for such minor items.

The most important fee for your purposes will be the termination fee. Most management companies require a specific term for their contracts. If you sell the property before the expiration of your agreement, you might have to pay a lump sum equal to the remaining management fee they might have earned. While such clauses are usually not negotiable, you can lessen their impact. Ask for an amendment so you will not owe the termination fee if one of their other owners buys your property. In the alternative, ask for a reduced termination fee. That way, the management company is motivated to tell their other owners about your house, because they keep the management account and they make the (reduced) termination fee from you.

How do I choose a good management company?

When interviewing property management firms, ask about their years of experience, and the experience of the current operations personnel. It does you no good to hire a management company that has been in business for twenty years if all line employees have little actual experience and no in-house training.

Inquire about how many units they manage and for how many different owners. A company that manages two hundred units might have one apartment complex owned by the firm itself. Find out how many single-family residences (houses) they manage, because the skills are completely different than managing apartments. If they will share the information with you, ask how many of their clients own more than six rental houses. A high number indicates a large pool of potential purchasers for your property. I also like to find out if the owners or managers of the company own rental houses. You have to decide how you feel about the answer—it might show experience and motivation. It might indicate their properties will get first shot at available tenants.

Ask for proof of liability insurance and for references. Actually check the references. You never know what current and former clients will say—often, they are brutally honest.

Be sure to ask for references who own rental houses. The client with a 500-unit apartment complex is not going to give you any good insights into how you will be treated. When talking to references, do not content yourself with a simple question like, "Do they do a good job for you?"

Here are some suggestions of questions you should ask references that will reveal valuable information.

- Who do you usually talk to at the management company?

- Assuming that person is an employee—if they left the company to open up their own management firm, would you move your business? Why?

- How long have you been a client of this company?

- Have you ever used another management company? What is better and worse about the one you have now?

- What do you wish the company did differently?

- What additional services do you wish they offered?

- How often are your properties vacant?

- How often do you raise your rents?

- Do you feel like your rents are equal to those charged in the marketplace? (A client who does not know has not been very well educated by the management firm.)

- When you call the company, can someone answer your questions immediately, or does someone have to call you back?

- How long does it take before you receive a return phone call?

- Have you had to make any repairs because of tenant damage? Can you tell me what happened?

- Have you had to evict anyone? Can you tell me what happened?

- Would you buy more rental houses if you found some good opportunities?

- Besides the regular fee you pay each month, what additional charges usually appear on your bill? How do you feel about those charges?

When interviewing the management company, inquire into the services they offer, and success stories in which they saved money for their clients or prevented problems. Stress you do not want any names, just some examples. Anyone who is good at what they do will have thought about these things and reflected on the good job they do for their clients. If the firm cannot share any success stories with you, you should think hard before doing business with them.

Ask for a few horror stories regarding other management firms or people who self-manage their rental properties. Again, be sure to mention that you do not want any names. A management firm that is in touch with its community will know those things. You want a management company that can justify the good it can do for you.

I usually ask each company what makes it better than its competition. Good firms have good, thoughtful responses to this question. Those are the ones you want to choose, as long as you can confirm that their responses are accurate. People who are not thoughtful about their business—and not serious about being in business—usually do not ask themselves such questions. People who trash their competition in very negative terms generally leave a bad taste in my mouth and I avoid them.

The national trade association for property managers is the Institute of Real Estate Management (IREM). Its website at **www.irem.org** includes a tab at the top of the page for owners/investors and information relevant to them.

If I manage my rental house myself, what issues might arise that are important to know about ahead of time?

The most important issues will be supervision and consistency. You cannot take an out of sight, out of mind attitude, satisfied with monthly rental checks and nothing more. Every good professional property manager knows three sayings by heart:

- The squeaky wheel gets the grease. (In other words, send out a bill reminding your tenant that the rent will be due. Call on the last day before the late charge will be assessed. Call every day after that if the rent is late. Demand a commitment for a date when the rent will be paid. Follow up on everything.)

- Inspect what you expect. (You cannot just hope everything is okay. Conduct regular property inspections. Drive by at unexpected times to see what the yard looks like and if there are any wild parties going on. Be present during all repairs, and make sure they are performed properly.)

- Don't date at the office. (Do not form personal friendships with your tenants because it will cloud your judgment and prevent you from taking a businesslike attitude towards things. You are more likely to listen to sad stories from friends about why they cannot pay their rent, month after month.)

What if my tenant does not pay the rent?

If your tenant does not pay the rent, you will have to evict him or her. Eviction laws vary widely from state to state. Check out Appendix E for resources that can give you local information.

In some states, eviction is a fairly speedy process that can be completed in about three weeks. In other states, especially if the tenants are experienced, they can prevent eviction for many months and even up to a year. Some states require the tenants to pay their monthly rent to the court in the meantime, until the disputes are resolved. Others do not.

You can minimize the likelihood of this kind of a problem if you keep excellent written records and if you keep all your commitments. Tenants who stall evictions for many months are able to do so because they make claims against their landlord. You might hear, "My landlord didn't fix the dripping faucet when he promised, and I couldn't sleep for weeks, and that caused me to lose my job, so my whole ruined life is the landlord's fault." Unfortunately, in an eviction situation, these types of accusations are not at all uncommon. Keep a journal for your rental house matters. Note all conversations with your tenant, including the date and approximate time. Include any complaints and promises by the tenant, and any responses and promises by you. Keep all of your promises exactly on time, and note the completion of them in your journal, as well. Make sure to follow up all conversations with a note or email confirming what you spoke about, and keep copies of all of these papers.

If there is a meltdown with your tenant and you end up in court, your journal might become valuable evidence. If it does become evidence, though, remember that it will be readable by everyone. This means that you should not vent your frustrations by calling your tenant names in the journal.

How do I prevent a tenant from damaging my property?

You can prevent damage by minimizing the opportunities for damage to occur in the first place. As previously mentioned, do not allow pets. Do not allow water beds. Limit occupants to no more than two people per bedroom. Cut down on party damage by setting a 10:00 p.m. limit on any parties. Do not allow parking on the lawn or backyard. Prohibit any cars without a current inspection sticker (if your state requires these), a current tag, and proof of insurance. Have a lease clause disallowing operating a business on the premises. Do not allow car repairs to be made on the property. Make it very clear in the lease that no matter how much your tenant thinks he or she might be improving the property, he or she cannot make any changes at all.

Finally, inspect the property on a regular basis. It keeps everyone on their best behavior. It presents opportunities for tenants to talk to you about the unit. Inspections also let you catch small problems early, before they turn into giant disasters. If you will make it a habit to inspect your house once a month, you will avoid a lot of potential problems.

What are my rights if my tenant files for Chapter 13 Bankruptcy?

At one time, Chapter 13 bankruptcy—the so-called wage earner's plan—was a landlord's worst nightmare. Sweeping legal changes that went into effect in 2005, changed this dramatically. Chapter 13 bankruptcy still allows a debtor to propose a payment plan for his or her past due debts, while also paying his or her current obligations on time. Creditors might not be paid in full for arrearages, and payments can be spread out over monthly payments for sixty months. On the other hand, landlords are given greater protections and can ask for permission to proceed with eviction under certain circumstances.

Debtors can file under other bankruptcy chapters, as well. Chapter 7 bankruptcy is for liquidations; Chapter 11 bankruptcy is a reorganization for businesses and for consumers with large debts; and, Chapter 12 bankruptcy is for family farmers. Each type of bankruptcy has its own rules and procedures. However, as a landlord, you are most likely to encounter Chapter 13 bankruptcy.

First, understand that when a person files for relief under Chapter 13, all collection activities must stop immediately by creditors who are listed on the bankruptcy petition. There are some exceptions, but caution is always best until you speak with a lawyer.

When confronted with a claim that someone has filed, ask for a case number and the name of his or her attorney, so you can confirm the information. You should also check the PACER (Public Access to Court Electronic Records) at **http://pacer.psc.uscourts.gov/** in order to see the actual documents, and find out whether or not you were listed as a creditor. Currently, the charge is 8¢ per page that you view, and there is no monthly access fee or subscription charge. If you are not listed as a creditor, your collection activities do not have to stop, even if you have actual knowledge of the bankruptcy filing.

If you are listed as a creditor on the bankruptcy petition, all collection efforts must stop immediately. You are not allowed to contact the debtor at all, except for routine matters not connected to collecting your debts. In a Chapter 13, if you have two or more tenants equally liable on the lease, but only one of them files for bankruptcy, you still must stop your collection activities against all of the tenants.

You will receive a notice from the court advising you of the date and time of the 341 Meeting, also called the First Meeting of the Creditors. Many other debtors will have their 341 Meeting scheduled for the same date and time. Come prepared to stay awhile, but leave your cell phone and other electronic devices in the car, because those are usually prohibited and may be confiscated when you go through security. Your 341 Meeting notice will also include important deadlines, including the date by which you must file your Proof of Claim.

The Chapter 13 Trustee will ask the debtor various routine questions about his or her financial affairs at the 341 Meeting. You will also have a chance to ask questions, but this is not a forum for grilling the debtor extensively. If you do not have an attorney, it might be best to tell the trustee your concerns about the property's condition, whether the tenant has renter's insurance, why there always seems to be eighteen people sleeping over, and other such issues. The trustee will then ask the appropriate questions for you.

Make sure you file your Proof of Claim form on time. A copy of the form can be found on the following page.

B 10 (Official Form 10) (12/07)

UNITED STATES BANKRUPTCY COURT	**PROOF OF CLAIM**

Name of Debtor:	Case Number:

NOTE: *This form should not be used to make a claim for an administrative expense arising after the commencement of the case. A request for payment of an administrative expense may be filed pursuant to 11 U.S.C. § 503.*

Name of Creditor (the person or other entity to whom the debtor owes money or property):

☐ Check this box to indicate that this claim amends a previously filed claim.

Name and address where notices should be sent:

Court Claim Number:_____
(*If known*)

Telephone number:

Filed on:_____

Name and address where payment should be sent (if different from above):

☐ Check this box if you are aware that anyone else has filed a proof of claim relating to your claim. Attach copy of statement giving particulars.

Telephone number:

☐ Check this box if you are the debtor or trustee in this case.

1. Amount of Claim as of Date Case Filed: $_____

If all or part of your claim is secured, complete item 4 below; however, if all of your claim is unsecured, do not complete item 4.

If all or part of your claim is entitled to priority, complete item 5.

☐ Check this box if claim includes interest or other charges in addition to the principal amount of claim. Attach itemized statement of interest or charges.

2. Basis for Claim:_____
(See instruction #2 on reverse side.)

3. Last four digits of any number by which creditor identifies debtor:_____

3a. Debtor may have scheduled account as:_____
(See instruction #3a on reverse side.)

4. Secured Claim (See instruction #4 on reverse side.)
Check the appropriate box if your claim is secured by a lien on property or a right of setoff and provide the requested information.

Nature of property or right of setoff: ☐ Real Estate   ☐ Motor Vehicle   ☐ Other
Describe:

Value of Property:$_____ **Annual Interest Rate**___%

Amount of arrearage and other charges as of time case filed included in secured claim,

if any: $_____ **Basis for perfection:**_____

Amount of Secured Claim: $_____ **Amount Unsecured: $**_____

6. Credits: The amount of all payments on this claim has been credited for the purpose of making this proof of claim.

7. Documents: Attach redacted copies of any documents that support the claim, such as promissory notes, purchase orders, invoices, itemized statements of running accounts, contracts, judgments, mortgages, and security agreements. You may also attach a summary. Attach redacted copies of documents providing evidence of perfection of a security interest. You may also attach a summary. (*See definition of "redacted" on reverse side.*)

DO NOT SEND ORIGINAL DOCUMENTS. ATTACHED DOCUMENTS MAY BE DESTROYED AFTER SCANNING.

If the documents are not available, please explain:

5. Amount of Claim Entitled to Priority under 11 U.S.C. §507(a). If any portion of your claim falls in one of the following categories, check the box and state the amount.

Specify the priority of the claim.

☐ Domestic support obligations under 11 U.S.C. §507(a)(1)(A) or (a)(1)(B).

☐ Wages, salaries, or commissions (up to $10,950*) earned within 180 days before filing of the bankruptcy petition or cessation of the debtor's business, whichever is earlier – 11 U.S.C. §507 (a)(4).

☐ Contributions to an employee benefit plan – 11 U.S.C. §507 (a)(5).

☐ Up to $2,425* of deposits toward purchase, lease, or rental of property or services for personal, family, or household use – 11 U.S.C. §507 (a)(7).

☐ Taxes or penalties owed to governmental units – 11 U.S.C. §507 (a)(8).

☐ Other – Specify applicable paragraph of 11 U.S.C. §507 (a)(___).

Amount entitled to priority:

$_____

Amounts are subject to adjustment on 4/1/10 and every 3 years thereafter with respect to cases commenced on or after the date of adjustment.

Date:	**Signature:** The person filing this claim must sign it. Sign and print name and title, if any, of the creditor or other person authorized to file this claim and state address and telephone number if different from the notice address above. Attach copy of power of attorney, if any.	FOR COURT USE ONLY

Penalty for presenting fraudulent claim: Fine of up to $500,000 or imprisonment for up to 5 years, or both. 18 U.S.C. §§ 152 and 3571.

If you do not file a Proof of Claim, you may be limited to the amount the debtor says he or she owes you, instead of the actual amount.

You may ask for permission to proceed with eviction under some circumstances, especially if you can show that the tenant is endangering the property or using illegal drugs on the premises. Under current law, landlords may also request a lifting of the automatic stay—permission to proceed with eviction—after thirty days have passed from the bankruptcy filing date. The debtor can oppose the request but has some tall hurdles to jump over. The law in this area is extremely technical, and is no time to save money with do-it-yourself, as you could find yourself in severe trouble with the court if you make a mistake. Hire a good lawyer with experience in residential landlord/tenant issues and bankruptcy.

Keep in mind, also, that a tenant in bankruptcy has the right to terminate what are called executory contracts. These are contracts that have continuing obligations, and include leases. In other words, your tenant can cancel their lease without penalty.

CONCLUSION

If I have done my job well, you now know the following.

1. Flipping houses is vastly different than the television shows and late-night infomercials would have you believe.

2. Flipping houses is far easier and much less risky than you secretly feared, and you can do it with a minimum amount of risk.

3. If you want to get rich quick, go to Vegas. If you want to build true wealth that will last your lifetime and provide income while you relax and do nothing, start flipping now to get started in real estate, and then use your profits to invest and hold for long-term rental income.

Let me know about your questions and experiences. I do answer emails! You can reach me at **flipping@deniselevans.com**.

Glossary

A

AAA-tenant. In speech, referred to as "triple-A tenant," but written as "AAA-tenant." A commercial tenant with the best possible credit rating and the least likely possibility of default. Owners can secure better selling prices or better financing terms if they have such tenants in their properties.

accrual method. An accounting method in which income is counted when it is earned (whether you receive the money at that time or not) and expenses are counted when incurred (whether you pay the bill at that time or not). It is the opposite of the cash method, in which income is counted when money is received and expenses are counted when the bills are paid. Most businesses use the accrual method because it allows income and the expenses associated with generating that income to be accounted for in the same period. The accrual method also usually provides better tax planning. Many small businesses use the cash method because it is easier.

ad valorem tax. Literally means "according to the value." It is a tax placed upon property and calculated with reference to the value of the property.

after-tax equity yield. Methods of financial analysis for an equity position in real estate, being the net return rate on an investment after deducting expenses, interest, and taxes. For example, an investor buys a property with $100,000 down (equity) and

$400,000 in financing. The investor receives $7,000 in cash flow each year, after paying income taxes on money earned from the investment. After five years, the investor sells the property and receives $150,000 after deducting taxes and sale costs. The investor receives a return of the original $100,000 and a sale profit of $50,000 upon sale, plus the $35,000 received over the course of five years, for a total of $85,000. After quantifying the various components, as above, you then calculate yield by using any of several formulas, such as cash-on-cash, internal rate of return, or any other method selected.

analysis paralysis. The condition that exists when you spend all your time analyzing deals, reading all the books you can, talking to insiders, and going to conventions and meetings, rather than actually doing a deal. Those with analysis paralysis generally do not want any risk at all. As a result, they constantly need just one more piece of information before deciding to go forward. Invariably, someone else eventually buys the property, and the person with analysis paralysis must look for something else.

appreciation. In the real world, most real estate increases in value over the years, or appreciates.

B

back of the envelope pro forma. An informal analysis of the costs associated with a project, the time period until you reach maximum gain, and the estimated sale price at that time, resulting in your net profits on a deal. It is called *back of the envelope* because such a rough estimate should be capable of calculation by jotting down items and numbers on the back of an old envelope.

basis. Tax and accounting term referring to the original acquisition cost (plus or minus adjustments made during the period of ownership) of a property. It is used to determine annual depreciation deductions and eventual gain or loss upon the disposition of the property. This concept is fundamental to almost all real estate analysis and real property tax planning, and an important one to master.

C

carrying charges. Costs incurred in owning property until it can be sold, as opposed to the costs of acquiring or rehabbing property. Carrying costs, also called holding costs, are things like utilities, insurance, yard maintenance, snow removal, and interest on your acquisition loan.

cash method. *See* accrual method.

change order. A written order from the owner, architect, engineer, or other authorized person to depart from previously agreed-upon plans and specifications for construction, rehab, or remodeling. Change order management is a critical aspect of any construction job, as change orders frequently change the cost of a job, usually in an amount far in excess of what novices might think. Many subcontractors bid prices at break-even prices, or even at a loss, in order to secure work. They are confident that numerous change orders will provide the profit they need. As an example, electricians might bid a job to perform all electrical wiring in a house at a rate equivalent to $15 per electrical outlet and electrical fixture. Add a few more outlets, though, and you might find out that the change orders cost $100 per outlet!

certificate of occupancy. Certificate from a government department, usually the inspections department, approving a building for use. If you do not obtain a certificate of occupancy when one is required, you can be prohibited from using your property or renting it out to anyone else.

credit bid. When a property is in foreclosure, this is the amount the lender agrees to credit the loan in return for receiving a deed.

D

deed of trust. A security instrument by which real estate secures a promissory note. In some states, this arrangement is a slightly different document, called a mortgage. *See also* mortgage.

deferred maintenance. Repairs that have been put off for a while and are starting to pile up.

depreciation. An accounting concept in which the IRS, and other people, pretend that assets will decrease steadily in value over a predetermined time period until, at the very end, they are completely worthless. It usually bears no relationship to reality, but does allow you to write off expenses on your taxes even though you are not actually writing checks for those expenses.

due diligence. The process of investigating all facts, conditions, rules, laws, regulations, financial considerations, or any other such matters as would affect one's decision to purchase property. The various types of investigations that would make up due diligence will vary from property to property. With the purchase of a home, it might include nothing more than a home inspection, termite report, and a review of any restrictive covenants. When purchasing raw land for development, it could include zoning issues, possible environmental contamination, surveys, an analysis of cost to develop versus value when completed, and so on.

E

earnest money. A deposit of money made by the purchaser of real estate. It can serve the following purposes.

1. Provide evidence of economic resources and the probable ability to proceed to closing.

2. Provide hostage value because of the usual contract provision that the seller may retain the earnest money in the event of default.

3. Allow enforcement of a contract that might be defective on purely technical grounds. For example, some states allow enforcement of an oral real estate contract when there has been partial performance by the payment of earnest money. This occurs often, as when a buyer submits a written offer for property and an earnest money check. The seller makes a verbal counteroffer and the buyer verbally accepts. The seller deposits the check. No one ever thinks to prepare a new written contract for signatures. Standing alone, this is an oral contract that is unenforceable under the statute of frauds.

electrical rough. Work performed by the electrical contractor after the plumber and heating contractor are finished. The electrical contractor usually receives a substantial payment on his or her contract price at the completion of the electrical rough.

electrical trim. Work performed by the electrical contractor when the house is nearing completion. The electrician installs all plugs, switches, light fixtures, smoke detectors, appliance pigtails, bath ventilation fans, wires the furnace, and makes up the electric house panel. The electrician does all work necessary to get the home ready for and to pass the municipal electrical final inspection.

eminent domain. The ability of the government to take property, whether the homeowner wants to sell or not.

equity. The difference between what a property is worth and what is owed on it. Just because someone pays $10,000 down to buy a property does not mean he or she has $10,000 worth of equity. If the property appreciated, then the equity will be larger. If the property declined in value, then the equity will be smaller.

equity stripping. A term applied to a variety of sleight-of-hand practices, most often:

- offering to assist homeowners facing foreclosure through buying their home and then selling it back to them, usually at rates and on terms guaranteed to result in default and loss of all equity; and,

- protecting assets from creditors by encumbering the equity with loans from friendly creditors, such as relatives, who will not foreclose if you miss a few payments.

F

fair market value. The price that a willing buyer would pay a willing seller, with neither of them operating under duress.

filled land. An area where the grade—the level of the land—has been raised, preferably by depositing clay, soil, rock, and gravel, and the fill has been compacted at regular intervals as the grade raised. Less ideal, but more common in areas with little regulatory oversight, is the practice of dumping tree stumps and other vegetation, covering them with six feet or so of clay, and then compacting only the top six feet. The property will pass most compaction studies, which bore down only six feet. In time, however, the vegetation will rot, the land will settle, and the owner will see potholes and foundation cracks.

first refusal, right of. The right to buy or rent real property if and when the owner decides to sell or lease. The owner is under no obligation to ever sell or lease, though. Contrast this with an option, in which the optionee (the person who wants to buy or lease) has a legal right to require the owner (optionor) to sell or lease, but the optionee does not have any obligation to buy or lease. With a right of first refusal, control is with the owner. With an option, control is with the potential buyer.

flip, assemblage. Buying options on several adjoining small parcels of property, and then selling them all in one large parcel for a profit.

flip, foreclosure owner. Buying property at a below-market price from sellers in economic difficulty and then reselling it for a profit.

flip, homeowner. Buying a house as your personal residence, fixing it up to increase its value, and selling it after two years.

flip, market rent. Buying a house to flip, cleaning it up to increase its value by a little bit, and selling it for a small profit.

flip, option. Buying an option on a piece of property and then selling your option for a small profit.

flip, parcel. Buying large parcels of property, breaking them up into smaller parcels of land, and then selling them at a larger per-acre or per-square-foot price.

flip, reservation. Signing a contract to buy property in a booming market, and then selling your contract to someone else at a profit.

flip, scrape. Buying a piece of land with an ugly, barely usable building on it, demolishing the building, and selling the vacant lot for a profit.

flip, television. Buying a house to flip, fixing it up to increase its value by a lot, and selling it for a large profit.

flip, under-market. Buying an option property from an owner who seriously undervalues his or her property, and then selling the property for a profit.

flip, vacancy. Buying a vacant rental house, putting a tenant in place, and selling it for a profit.

flipping. Gaining control of real estate for a short period of time with the intention of selling it to someone else for a profit.

for-sale-by-owner (FSBO). Homes being sold by the seller without a real estate agent.

G

gentrification. The informal process of revitalizing an older and deteriorated neighborhood into more upscale homes owned by more affluent occupants. The first step is usually taken by young professionals seeking affordable housing in an urban setting, who immediately begin using disposable income to upgrade their properties. Their efforts attract other like-minded homebuyers. Eventually the neighborhood reaches a point where the existing homeowners can afford to sell their properties and buy elsewhere, but cannot afford to pay the increasing property taxes. The process gains momentum at that point, with former apartment buildings converted to condos, single-family residences undergoing complete renovations, and the entire neighborhood changing to middle class or upper-middle class status.

guarantee. The act itself, or the document, whereby one agrees to pay a debt if the principal obligor does not. Under common law, creditors had to exhaust their remedies against a debtor before pursuing a guarantor. Today, almost all guarantee instruments contain clauses allowing the creditor to seek payment directly from the guarantor if there has been a default by the debtor. Guarantee agreements must be in writing to be enforceable. There must be some consideration passing to the guarantor unless the instrument creating the obligation (i.e., the lease) is signed at the same time as the guarantee, in which case the law assumes the guarantor has some interest in the transaction.

H

handyman's special. In real estate advertising, this generally indicates a building with substantial deterioration and in need of extensive repairs beyond normal painting or fix-up aesthetic improvement.

holding costs. *See* carrying charges.

L

LIBOR (pronounced lie-bore). *London InterBank Offered Rate.* The rate that banks around the world use to charge interest to each other on large loans with terms from twenty-four hours to five years. LIBOR is used as an index for many commercial loans in the United States, rather than a reference to *prime rate.* In recent years, LIBOR has been about 3%–4% less than quoted prime rates. Lenders who quote commercial loan rates based on LIBOR will usually say something similar to "150 basis points over one-year LIBOR." If LIBOR on one-year bank-to-bank loans is currently at 5.25%, then the quoted loan rate for the customer will be 5.25% plus 1.50%, or 6.75% By comparison, a loan quoted at "1.5% over prime" might cost 9% interest, because prime might be 7.5%.

lien. A generic name for claims against real estate. Lien holders can hold mortgages, they can be creditors who filed judgments, or they might be taxing authorities like the IRS or your local government.

M

mechanics' and materialmen's liens. Statutory lien granted in some states to specifically describe persons who provide goods or services contributing to the improvement of real property under a contract with the owner or the owner's representative, such as a general contractor. The lien will attach in favor of subcontractors even if the owner paid the general contractor, but the general contractor did not pay the subcontractors. It can take priority over a mortgage if the work was started before the mortgage was recorded, even if the lien document was not filed until after the mortgage was filed. Most statutes grant a very short time after nonpayment for the lien documents to be filed, or the lien will be lost. After that, the person claiming under the lien must promptly take steps to foreclose his or her lien, or it will be lost. Property owners may protect themselves in some states by posting notices of nonresponsibility on the property, advising all subcontractors and vendors that they must look only to the general contractor for payment.

mortgage. A security instrument by which real estate secures a promissory note. In some states, this arrangement is a slightly different document called a deed of trust.

O

option. The right to purchase or lease property for an agreed-upon price. The person who owns the property is called the *optionor*, and is the one who grants the option. The recipient of the option is called the *optionee*. The parties must have an agreed-upon price or a firm method of calculating the price. The option must also be for a finite period of time. The optionee has the right to take advantage of the opportunity, but does not have the obligation to do so. In most states, the optionee must pay some consideration for the purchase of the option right, or the optionee must have received the option in connection with its lease of the property. If not, the option contract is not enforceable. *See also* first refusal, right of.

P

Phase I Environmental Report. A report prepared by an enniron-
mental engineer that deatils the historical use of specific property
and surrounding properties, the existence of nearby hazardous
waste sites, and the results of interviews with neighbors and
former owners. The purpose of this report is to evaluate the likelihood that hazardous waste might be present. The engineer
performs no actual testing for this report. If the Phase I Report
indicates that hazardous products might be present, then a lender
will usually require a Phase II Report, which is prepared after
actual soil and water testing.

profit. Net income that you pay taxes on. Because the principal
portion of mortgage payments do not qualify as an accounting or
an IRS expense, you can have a paper profit but still not have
enough money to pay your bills.

S

sweat equity. Increase in value of property due to the rehabilitation
and renovation efforts of the owner, usually acting as his or her
own general contractor, subcontractor, and laborer.

T

tax-free exchange. A tax break available to investors. If you are an
investor, the IRS says that you do not have to pay income taxes in
the current year on your profits if you sell one property, buy
another property of equal or greater value, and invest all your cash
from the first sale in the purchase of the second property.

title insurance. An insurance policy that pays off if it turns out that
you do not have good and clear title to your property. Title insur-

ance typically does not cover boundary line disputes or adverse possession claims. Lenders always require title insurance, but many buyers do not think to ask for coverage for themselves, as well.

Torrens certificate. Instrument issued by the registrar of legal titles in a state that employs the optional Torrens system for title registration. The certificate operates much like a car title, listing the name of the owner and any mortgage or deed of trust liens, plus any other liens or encumbrances. *See also* Torrens registration.

Torrens registration. The process of first entering a property into the optional land registration system known as the Torrens system. For the states and counties that offer this as an alternative to the more traditional abstract method, registration begins as a lawsuit. The property owner sets out all the evidence showing its entitlement to the property and any mortgages or other liens against the property. The owner must disclose other persons who might have a claim to the same property. Those persons receive notice of the suit. There is usually also a method of public notice in case other claimants wish to assert their rights. Normally, no other claimant disputes the title and the court orders issuance of a Torrens certificate. If there is a dispute, the lawsuit will proceed just like any other suit, with a trial and a decision.

SAMPLE LOAN REQUEST

(Note: All numbers are invented. Do not use this as a guide for your anticipated expenses)

John and Sally Smith request a loan in the amount of $200,000 to buy and renovate a house located at 1012 Maple Street, Springville, Kansas. The loan will be secured by a first mortgage on the property.

The house can be purchased for $150,000 and will require an additional $50,000 for expenses and holding costs until completion and sale, estimated to be six months from the date of purchase.

They are requesting a nine-month loan to allow some extra time for unanticipated delays.

The renovation budget is as follows. (Where available, firm bids or subcontractor quotes are attached to this loan request.)

Dumpster rental and debris removal	$1,000
Interior paint	4,500
Exterior brick cleaning	2,500
Carpentry repairs, build deck	4,000
Plumbing labor and fixtures	6,000
Electrical labor and fixtures	4,500
Carpet replacement	8,000
Utilities	3,000
Construction period interest	8,000
Insurance	1,000
Permits	1,500
Contingencies	6,000
Total	$50,000

Comparable homes in this neighborhood typically sell for $375,000 after three months on the market. Information regarding comparable sales is attached to this Request.

SAMPLE HOUSE FLIPPING BUSINESS PLAN

[Note: All numbers are invented. Do not think this is how much it costs to do a housekeeping flip. Everyone's budget will be different.]

Goal: To buy and sell one housekeeping flip every three months for the next three years. In Year One, each housekeeping flip must net me $5,000 in profit after paying all expenses. In Year Two, my profit must be $6,500 per flip, and in Year Three, my profit must be at least $8,000 per flip.

Budget per house: $3,800 and 216 hours of labor, working out to an average of 18 hours per week.

[Note: Once you calculate your time requirements, divide the profit you require by the time it will take. In this case, you require $5,000 in profit and it will cost you 216 hours. That works out to $23.15 per hour. Is that a good return for your time? If not, revise your plan or do something different.]

- An average of 5 hours per week in general continuing education about the marketplace and about flipping
- 40 hours to find the right opportunity
- 32 hours for interior and exterior cleaning and minor yard work
- 8 hours for minor repairs

- 16 hours for painting
- $500 for cleaning supplies, small tools, and repair items
- $3,000 for holding costs, including interest, insurance, taxes, utilities, lawn care, and snow removal
- $300 for debris removal
- 60 hours for marketing efforts, showings, negotiations, and any preclosing chores or tasks

Equipment needs: I will use the profits from the first house to buy electric painting equipment, a good quality carpet shampoo machine, a used pressure washer, step ladder, and bulk quantities of frequently needed items like switch plate covers, off-white paint, sheet rock mud, and garbage bags.

Space needs: I will need a dedicated area to keep all my how-to books, market information, leads, and business records. I will convert the hall coat closet into a locker for my stuff. I will also need a three-foot by eight-foot section of the garage for my cleaning and repair supplies, and I will rope it off if I need to so my material stays separate from everything else.

Business aids: I will need a good purchase contract form that I can revise easily myself, if necessary. I will also need an inspection checklist, a filing system for information about comparable properties, and index cards or some other system for keeping track of potential purchases. I will need a phone number that people can call and leave messages for me, without running the risk that my spouse or children will accidentally erase my messages. I will need a specific time each week when I can count on using the family computer, my own computer, or a paper system that helps me keep up with all information, including time and money expenditures. *[Note: Pick one that works for you; do not list all three systems in your business plan.]*

Market area: I will concentrate my efforts in the school district where my children attend elementary school.

Type of house: I have learned that three-bedroom, two-bathroom, brick, single-story houses typically stay on the market three months or less in my area, and it makes no difference if there is a real estate agent involved or not. I will look for houses meeting that profile.

Price range: I have the ability to borrow up to $75,000 and still keep the interest payments within the overall monthly budget I established for myself, and I can afford to pay $10,000 in a down payment. *[Note: If you plan to take money out of an income-earning vehicle like a savings account in order to use it as a down payment, you must include the lost interest income as one of your expenses in your budget. Making a $2,000 profit on a house makes no sense if your expenses are $1,300 and you lose $800 of interest because you took money out of savings for a down payment.]*

Finding inventory: In order to find potential deals, I will spend two hours a week driving, walking, or bicycling around my market area to keep an eye out for old and faded "for sale" signs, new "for sale" signs in messy yards, or piles of rubbish set out on the curb as if someone were getting ready to move. I will also spend another twenty minutes per day, every day, talking to different people to find leads. I will have no less than fourteen people I talk to, so that I do not bother anyone more than twice a month.

Family involvement: I will involve my family in this project. My family has agreed that they will all work *together* at least six hours per house to help me clean it. They have also agreed that during my designated office hours of 8 p.m. to 9 p.m. each night, Monday through Thursday, they will pretend I do not exist and they will fend for themselves.

Marketing plan to sell houses: I will hold an open house and invite all the neighbors in a _[X]_ block area. They are my most likely sources for the names of people who want to move into that area. I will also put flyers on the bulletin boards of all grocery stores, day care centers, and churches in my market area. I will identify everyone who owns rental houses in my area, so I can see if they would like to buy more. [Note: You get the idea. List all the things you will do to market each and every house. If you have a list, you have much better odds of actually doing the right things, and selling the house.]

Taxes: As soon as I sell a house, I will immediately put _[X]_% of the profits into a savings account to be used when I will have to pay income taxes on my profits. [Note: Be sure to carefully read the questions on taxes in Chapter 2. You may have to pay taxes at ordinary income rates rather than capital gains rates, and you might have to pay self-employment taxes for Social Security and Medicare.]

Appendix C

CHECKLIST OF CONSTRUCTION, REHAB, AND RENOVATION EXPENSE CATEGORIES

Use this form as a checklist to start thinking about the right expense areas. It is by no means exhaustive. Add other categories as you think of them.

GENERAL REQUIREMENTS

- Allowances
  - ❑ Marketing package design
  - ❑ Reproducibles, plans, copies, mailings, etc.
- Project coordination
  - ❑ Construction project management
  - ❑ Field office setup & supplies
- Insurance expense
  - ❑ General liability
  - ❑ Builder's risk
  - ❑ Equipment rental
  - ❑ Workers' compensation
- Field engineering
  - ❑ Boundary line/As-built survey
  - ❑ Topographical survey

❑Building/site layout design

❑Mechanical & electrical engineering

- Regulatory requirements

  ❑Building permit costs

  ❑Municipality licensing requirements for subs

- Temporary utilities

  ❑Electric, phone, water, & portable toilets

  ❑Utility connection costs

  ❑Startup deposits

- Temporary construction

  ❑Staging areas & tool security

- Project Signage

- Material & equipment—transportation & handling

  ❑Dumpsters

  ❑Hauling fees

  ❑Material handling costs

- Final cleaning

- Small tools

SITE WORK

- Geotechnical & environmental reports

- General demolition

- Site clearing

  ❑Tree removal

- Earthwork

  ❑Rough grading

  ❑Fine grading

- Paving & surfacing

  ❑Concrete

  ❑Asphalt

- Sidewalks

- Curbs & gutters
- Storm water systems
    - ❏ Catch basins
    - ❏ Culverts
    - ❏ Underground drainage pipe
    - ❏ Erosion & sediment control (during construction)
- Sanitary sewer system
    - ❏ Sewage collection lines
    - ❏ Septic tanks
- Fences & gates
    - ❏ Chain link fencing
    - ❏ Chain link gates
    - ❏ Decorative fencing
    - ❏ Decorative gates
- Walk & road accessories
- Landscaping

CONCRETE
- Formwork
    - ❏ Foundation repair
    - ❏ Retaining walls
    - ❏ Slab repair
    - ❏ Staircases, landings, columns, accessories
- Concrete reinforcing
    - ❏ Reinforcing steel
    - ❏ Welded wire fabric
    - ❏ Mesh
    - ❏ Stressing tendons
- Structural concrete
    - ❏ Foundations
    - ❏ Retaining walls

❑Slabs

❑Staircases, landings, columns, accessories

- Curing & finishing
- Tilt-up panels
- Cementitious decks
- Lightweight concrete

MASONRY

- Brick masonry
  ❑Brick
  ❑Mortar
  ❑Labor
  ❑Inbeds
  ❑Equipment rental
- Concrete block masonry
  ❑Concrete block
  ❑Dry-block additives
  ❑Mortar
  ❑Labor
  ❑Inbeds
  ❑Equipment rental

METALS

- Structural metal framing
- Metal fabrications
- Metal stairs
- Handrails & railings
- Ornamental metals

WOOD & PLASTICS

- Rough carpentry

❏Wood framing

❏Wood sheathing

❏Wood decking

•Finish carpentry

•Millwork & cabinets

•Ornamental woodwork

THERMAL & MOISTURE PROTECTION

•Waterproofing

❏Roll-on, polyethylene sheeting (non-metal walls)

•Vapor barriers

❏Walls

❏Slabs

❏Roofs

•Insulation

❏Walls

❏Roofing

•Shingles & roofing

•Flashing & sheet metal

•Sheet metal roofing

DOORS & WINDOWS

•Metal doors & frames

•Wood doors & frames

•Wood doors (hollow core)

•Specialty doors

•Metal windows

•Wood & plastic windows

•Door hardware

•Glazing

FINISHES

- Aggregate coatings
- Gypsum board (sheet rock)
- Tile applications (other than floors)
  - ❑ Ceramic tile
  - ❑ VCT
- Acoustical ceilings
  - ❑ Indoor
  - ❑ Outdoor
- Acoustical wall treatment
- Flooring
  - ❑ Tile
  - ❑ Carpet
  - ❑ Wood/bamboo/cork
  - ❑ Sheet vinyl
  - ❑ Laminate
- Countertops
  - ❑ Tile
  - ❑ Laminate
  - ❑ Hard natural surface (granite, etc.)
  - ❑ Hard composite surface (Corian, etc.)
- Painting
  - ❑ Exterior
  - ❑ Interior
- Wall coverings

SPECIALTIES

- Pest control
- Awnings
- Canopies
- Carport/garage

- Recreational areas
- Bath specialties (sauna, etc.)

EQUIPMENT RENTAL

FURNISHINGS
- Window treatments
- Furniture & accessories
- Rugs & mats

SPECIAL CONSTRUCTION
- Special purpose rooms
  - ❑ Specialty storage issues
- Pre-engineered fireplace

CONVEYING SYSTEMS
- Elevators
  - ❑ Hydraulic
  - ❑ Cable & pulley
- Lifts
  - ❑ Fixed
  - ❑ Mobile
- Material handling systems
  - ❑ Conveyor belts
  - ❑ Dumbwaiters
  - ❑ Forklifts
  - ❑ Pallet jacks
  - ❑ Carts & dollies

MECHANICAL
- Fire protection

- ❑Sprinkler system
- ❑Fire plug
- •Plumbing
  - ❑Piping
  - ❑Fixtures
  - ❑Equipment
- •HVAC systems
  - ❑Split systems
  - ❑Heat pumps
  - ❑Straight cool w/ strip heat
  - ❑Duct work
- •Control systems

ELECTRICAL

- •Electric service & distribution
- •Transformer
- •Lighting fixtures
  - ❑Exterior
  - ❑Interior
- •Appliances
  - ❑Cooking
  - ❑Refrigeration
  - ❑Dishwashing
  - ❑Venting/exhaust
- •Communications
  - ❑Telephone systems
  - ❑Alarm systems
  - ❑Intercom systems
  - ❑Computer network systems
  - ❑Television systems

Appendix D SOURCES OF INFORMATION ABOUT POTENTIAL FLIP OPPORTUNITIES

Houses in need of repairs

- Fire, flood, and disaster recovery and cleanup services such as ServPro

- Insurance agents

- Professional handymen who are often asked to look at projects too large for them to handle

- Plumbers, electricians, and carpenters who are asked to give quotes and then not hired because the homeowner cannot afford them

- Fire department records of uninsured fire losses

- Social service agencies for the elderly

- Housekeeping services (Many people will pay for cleaning services before they will pay for repairs. The housekeepers see the declining condition of the property, week in and week out.)

- Local government condemnation orders (These are generally large projects, which is why the properties are deemed unsafe. Sometimes, however, all they need is a new roof and replaced flooring.)

- Real estate agents who list properties advertised as *fixer-uppers*. (Often, such listings will have expired by the time you start looking, but the agent knows the owner is still willing to sell, at an attractive price. The owner is probably also still willing to pay the agent a commission.)

- Rental properties with rents significantly below market rate. (There is usually a reason the rents are so low. It is either because the owner does not know where the market is, or the property is in bad shape and will not bring market rates.)

Rental properties that cannot keep tenants
- Locksmiths (This is because many landlords change the locks every time they change tenants.)

- Classified ads (For this, you will need to keep track of the houses advertised for rent, and how long the ads run.)

- Online blogs that post complaints about local landlords

Sellers in economic distress
- Lenders (I know, they are not supposed to gossip, but many do.)

- Preforeclosure notices (For your state's foreclosure procedures, with the early warning signs, visit the RealtyTrac website at **www.realtytrac.com/education/noframes/foreclosurePro.html**.)

- Post-foreclosure properties:

  - www.hud.gov/homes/homesforsale.cfm
  - www.foreclosurelistings.com
  - www.foreclosure.com
  - www.foreclosurefreesearch.com

REAL ESTATE INFORMATION BY STATE

Alabama

Consumer Protection: www.ago.state.al.us/consumer.cfm

Disclosures: Alabama does not have state-specific disclosure laws and is, instead, a *caveat emptor* (buyer beware) state regarding sales of used property.

General Information: www.arerec.cba.ua.edu

Landlord/Tenant: http://ali.state.al.us/legislation/landlord_ tenant.pdf

Local HUD Information: www.hud.gov/local/index.cfm?state=al

Real Estate Commission: www.arec.alabama.gov

Alabama Center for Real Estate: www.arerec.cba.ua.edu

University of South Alabama Real Estate Center: www.southalabama.edu/publicrelations/pressreleases/2005pr/091205.html

Alaska

Consumer Protection: www.law.state.ak.us/department/civil/consumer/cp_index_template.html

Disclosures: www.dced.state.ak.us/occ/pub/rec4229.pdf

Landlord/Tenant: www.hud.gov/local/ak/renting/tenantrights.cfm

Local HUD Information: www.hud.gov/local/index.cfm?state=ak

Real Estate Commission: www.dced.state.ak.us/occ/prec.htm

Arizona

Department of Real Estate: www.re.state.az.us

Disclosures: www.re.state.az.us/PUBLIC_INFO/Documents/ Residential_Seller_Property_Disclosure_Statement.pdf

www.aaronline.com/documents/spds_samp.pdf

Landlord/Tenant: www.hud.gov/local/az/renting/tenantrights.cfm

Helpful links: www.keytlaw.com/az/realestate/relawlinks.htm

Local HUD Information: www.hud.gov/local/index.cfm?state=az

Residential Landlord/Tenant Law: www.azsos.gov/public_services/ publications/Residential_Landlord_Tenant_Act

Arizona State University: www.poly.asu.edu/realty

Arkansas

Local HUD Information: www.hud.gov/local/index.cfm?state=ar

Real Estate Commission: www.state.ar.us/arec/arecweb.html

California

Department of Fair Employment and Housing: www.dfeh.ca.gov

Department of Real Estate: www.dre.cahwnet.gov

Landlord/Tenant Law: www.hud.gov/local/ca/renting/tenantrights.cfm

Local HUD Information: www.hud.gov/local/index.cfm?state=ca

California Department of Real Estate, Disclosures in Real Property Transactions: www.dre.ca.gov/pub_disclosures.html

California Department of Real Estate (with guides and information for consumers): www.dre.ca.gov

University of California (Berkley): http://groups.haas.berkeley. edu/realestate/

University of Southern California: www.usc.edu/schools/sppd/ lusk/

Colorado

Consumer Protection: www.ago.state.co.us/consprot/
CoResourceGuide.cfm

Division of Real Estate: www.dora.state.co.us/real-estate/index.htm

General: www.hud.gov/local/co/renting/tenantrights.cfm

Landlord/Tenant Law: www.bouldercolorado.gov/index.php?
option=com_content&task=view&id=3767&Itemid=1406

Local HUD Information: www.hud.gov/local/index.cfm?
state=co

University of Colorado: http://leeds.colorado.edu/realestate/
index.aspx?id=295,247

Connecticut

Consumer Protection: www.ct.gov/dcp/site/default.asp

Division of Real Estate and Real Estate Appraisal: www.dora.
state.co.us/real-estate

Landlord/Tenant Law Law: www.jud.ct.gov/faq/landlord.html

Local HUD Information: www.hud.gov/local/index.cfm?state=ct

Residential Property Disclosure Report: www.ct.gov/
dcp/lib/dcp/pdf/realestate_licensing_forms/disclose.pdf

University of Connecticut: www.business.uconn.edu/cms/cms/p266

Delaware

Consumer protection: http://attorneygeneral.delaware.gov

Disclosures: http://delcode.delaware.gov/title6/c025/sc07/index.
shtml

General: www.hud.gov/local/de/renting/tenantrights.cfm

Landlord/Tenant Law: http://attorneygeneral.delaware.gov/
consumers/protection/brochure/landlordcode.pdf

Local HUD Information: www.hud.gov/local/index.cfm? state=de

Real Estate Commission: http://dpr.delaware.gov/boards/realestate/index.shtml

District of Columbia

Consumer Protection: http://app.dcra.dc.gov/information/ build_pla/ occupational/real_estate/index.shtm

Fair Housing: http://ohr.dc.gov/ohr/cwp/view,a,3,q,627574, ohrNav,%7C30953%7C.asp

Landlord/Tenant Law: http://dcra.dc.gov/dcra/frames.asp?doc=/ dcra/lib/dcra/information/forms_docs/pdf/tenantguide.pdf& group=1697&open=%7C33466%7C

Local HUD Information: www.hud.gov/local/index.cfm?state= dc

Florida

Consumer Protection: http://myfloridalegal.com/consumer

General: www.hud.gov/local/fl/renting/tenantrights.cfm

Landlord/Tenant Law: www.800helpfla.com/landlord_text.html

Local HUD Information: www.hud.gov/local/index.cfm?state=fl

Real Estate Commission: www.myflorida.com/dbpr/re/frec_ welcome.shtml

Florida State University: www.cob.fsu.edu/rmi/reecenter/ctr_ree. cfm

University of Florida: www.cba.ufl.edu/fire/realestate

Georgia

Consumer Protection: www.georgia.gov/00/channel_title/0, 2094,4802_5041,00.html

Fair Housing: www.gceo.state.ga.us/housing.htm

General: www.hud.gov/local/ga/renting/tenantrights.cfm

Landlord/Tenant Law: www.dca.state.ga.us/housing/Housing Development/programs/downloads/landlord/contents.html

Local HUD Information: www.hud.gov/local/index.cfm?state=ga

Real Estate Commission: www.grec.state.ga.us

University of Georgia: www.terry.uga.edu/realestate

Georgia State University: http://robinson.gsu.edu/realestate/rerc/index.html

Hawaii

Consumer Protection: www.hawaii.gov/dcca/areas/ocp

Fair Housing: www.hud.gov/local/hi/homeownership/fairhsg.cfm

General: www.hud.gov/local/hi/renting/tenantrights.cfm

Landlord/Tenant Law: www.hawaii.gov/dcca/areas/ocp/landlord_tenant

Local HUD Information: www.hud.gov/local/index.cfm?state=hi

Real Estate Branch: www.hawaii.gov/hirec

Idaho

Consumer Protection: http://www2.state.id.us/ag/consumer/

Disclosures: http://www3.state.id.us/idstat/TOC/55025KTOC.html

Fair Housing: www.ihfa.org/research_fairhousing.asp

General: www.hud.gov/local/id/renting/tenantrights.cfm

Landlord/Tenant Law: http://www2.state.id.us/ag/consumer/
tips/LandlordTenant.pdf

Local HUD Information: www.hud.gov/local/index.cfm?state=ia

Real Estate Commission: www.idahorealestatecommission.com

Illinois

Consumer Protection: www.illinoisattorneygeneral.gov/consumers/
index.html

Disclosures: www.illinoisrealtor.org/iar/buy_sell/legal/
disclosure.html

Fair Housing: www.state.il.us/dhr/Housenet/index.html

Landlord/Tenant Law: www.hud.gov/local/il/renting/
tenantrights.cfm

www.chicityclerk.com/legislation/codes/chapter5_12.pdf

Local HUD Information: www.hud.gov/local/index.cfm?state=il

Bureau of Real Estate Professions: www.idfpr.com/dpr/RE/
realmain.asp

DePaul University: http://realestate.depaul.edu/index.htm

University of Illinois: www.business.uiuc.edu/orer

Northwestern University: www.kellogg.northwestern.edu/academic/
realestate/index.htm

Indiana

Consumer Protection: www.in.gov/attorneygeneral/consumer

Disclosures: www.in.gov/icpr/webfile/formsdiv/46234.pdf

Fair Housing: www.in.gov/icrc/fairhousing

Landlord/Tenant Law: www.hud.gov/local/in/renting/
tenantrights.cfm

Local HUD Information: www.hud.gov/local/index.cfm?state=in

Real Estate Commission: www.in.gov/pla/bandc/estate
Indiana University: www.indiana.edu/~cres/realestate

Iowa

Consumer Protection: www.state.ia.us/government/ag

Disclosures: www.legis.state.ia.us/IACODE/2003/558A

Fair Housing: www.iowarealtors.com/consumers/equal.htm

Landlord/Tenant Law: www.hud.gov/local/ia/renting/tenantrights.
cfm

Local HUD Information: www.hud.gov/local/index.cfm?state=ia

Real Estate Commission: www.state.ia.us/government/com/
prof/sales/home.html

Kansas

Consumer Protection: www.ksag.org/content/page/id/39

Disclosures: www.kansasrealtor.com/secure/contracts/
residential/propdisc.pdf

Fair Housing: www.khrc.net

Landlord/Tenant Law: www.hud.gov/local/ks/renting/tenantrights.
cfm

Local HUD Information: www.hud.gov/local/index.cfm?state=ks

Real Estate Commission: www.accesskansas.org/krec

Wichita State University: http://realestate.wichita.edu/research.
asp

Kentucky

Consumer Protection: www.kentucky.gov/Portal/Category/hea_
consumer

Disclosures: www.lrc.state.ky.us/kar/201/011/350.htm
Fair Housing: www.kyhousing.org
Landlord/Tenant Law: www.hud.gov/local/ky/renting/tenantrights.
cfm
Local HUD Information: www.hud.gov/local/index.cfm?state=ky
Real Estate Commission: www.krec.ky.gov
University of Kentucky: http://gatton.uky.edu/CRES/Index.html

Louisiana

Consumer Protection: www.ag.state.la.us/ConsumerProtection.
aspx
Disclosures: www.lrec.state.la.us/forms.htm#residential
Fair Housing: www.lafairhousing.org
Landlord/Tenant Law: www.ag.state.la.us/publications/
landlord.htm
Local HUD Information: www.hud.gov/local/index.cfm?state=la
Real Estate Commission: www.lrec.state.la.us
Louisiana State University: www.bus.lsu.edu/centers/reri

Maine

Consumer Protection: www.maine.gov/ag/?r=protection
Disclosures: http://janus.state.me.us/legis/statutes/33/
title 33sec173.html
Fair Housing: www.maine.gov/mhrc/publications/fair_housing.
html
Landlord/Tenant Law: www.hud.gov/local/me/renting/tenantrights.
cfm
Local HUD Information: www.hud.gov/local/index.cfm? state= me
Real Estate Commission: www.maine.gov/pfr/

professionallicensing/index.shtml

University of Southern Maine: http://cree.usm.maine.edu/

Maryland

Consumer Protection: www.oag.state.md.us/Consumer/index.htm

Disclosures: www.dllr.state.md.us/forms/danddform.doc

Fair Housing: www.mchr.state.md.us

Landlord/Tenant Law: www.hud.gov/local/md/renting/tenantrights.cfm

Local HUD Information: www.hud.gov/local/index.cfm?state=md

Real Estate Commission: www.dllr.state.md.us/license/occprof/recomm.html

Massachusetts

Consumer Protection: www.ago.state.ma.us

Disclosures: www.mass.gov/legis/laws/mgl/111-197a.htm

Fair Housing: www.massfairhousing.org/joomla/index.php?option=com_wrapper&Itemid=36

Landlord/Tenant Law: www.hud.gov/local/ma/renting/ tenantrights.cfm

Local HUD Information: www.hud.gov/local/index.cfm?state=ma

Real Estate Commission: www.mass.gov

Harvard University: www.jchs.harvard.edu

Massachusetts Institute of Technology: http://web.mit.edu/cre/index.html

Michigan

Consumer Protection: www.michigan.gov/ag

Disclosures: http://law.justia.com/michigan/codes/mcl-chap565/mcl-act-92-of-1993.html

Fair Housing: www.fairhousinginmichigan.org

Landlord/Tenant Law: www.hud.gov/local/mi/renting/tenantrights.cfm

Local HUD Information: www.hud.gov/local/index.cfm?state=mi

Real Estate Commission: www.michigan.gov/cis/0,1607,7-154-35299_35414_35475-114980—,00.html

Forms located at:

www.cis.state.mi.us/dms/results.asp?docowner=BCSC&doccat=Real+Estate&Search=Search

Real Estate Law Book: www.michigan.gov/documents/cis/redbook_revised_February_2007-1_187962_7.pdf

Minnesota

Consumer Protection: www.ag.state.mn.us

Disclosures: www.mnrealtor.com/forms/faq/asis.html

Fair Housing: www.mnhousing.gov/about/fair-housing/index.asp

Landlord/Tenant Law: www.hud.gov/local/mn/renting/tenantrights.cfm

Local HUD Information: www.hud.gov/local/index.cfm?state=mn

Department of Commerce (Real Estate): www.state.mn.us/portal/mn/jsp/content.do?subchannel=-536881389&id=-536881352&agency=Commerce

Mississippi

Consumer Protection: www.ago.state.ms.us/divisions/consumer

Disclosures: www.mrec.ms.gov/docs/
mrec_forms_property_condition_disclosure.pdf

Fair Housing: www.msbar.org/10_you_and_your_home.php?
spot=1199&archive=19

Landlord/Tenant Law: www.hud.gov/local/ms/renting/tenantrights.
cfm

Local HUD Information: www.hud.gov/local/index.cfm?state=ms

Real Estate Commission: www.mrec.ms.gov

Missouri

Consumer Protection: www.ago.mo.gov/divisions/
consumerprotection.htm

Fair Housing: www.moga.mo.gov/statutes/c200-299/
2130000040.htm

Landlord/Tenant Law: www.hud.gov/local/mo/renting/ tenantrights.
cfm

Local HUD Information: www.hud.gov/local/index.cfm?state=mo

Real Estate Commission: http://pr.mo.gov/realestate.asp

Montana

Consumer Protection: www.doj.mt.gov/consumer

Fair Housing: www.fairhousing.montana.com

Landlord/Tenant Law: www.hud.gov/local/mt/renting/tenantrights.cfm

Local HUD Information: www.hud.gov/local/index.cfm?state=mt

Board of Realty Regulation: http://commerce.state.mt.us

Nebraska

Consumer Protection: www.ago.state.ne.us/consumer

Disclosures: www.sos.state.ne.us/rules-and-regs/regsearch/Rules/Real_Estate_Commission/Title-302/Chapter-1.pdf

Fair Housing: www.neoc.ne.gov/laws/hsng.htm

Landlord/Tenant Law: www.hud.gov/local/ne/renting/tenantrights.cfm

Local HUD Information: www.hud.gov/local/index.cfm?state=ne

Real Estate Commission: www.nrec.state.ne.us

Nevada

Consumer Protection: http://ag.state.nv.us/org/bcp/bcp.htm

Disclosures: http://red.state.nv.us/forms/547.pdf

Fair Housing: www.nfhc.org

Landlord/Tenant Law: www.hud.gov/local/nv/renting/tenantrights.cfm

Local HUD Information: www.hud.gov/local/index.cfm?state=nv

Real Estate Division: www.red.state.nv.us

New Hampshire

Consumer Protection: http://doj.nh.gov/consumer

Disclosures: www.nh.gov/nhrec/adrule2f.html#rea701

Fair Housing: www.nhla.org/nhlafhp.php

Landlord/Tenant Law: www.hud.gov/local/nh/renting/tenantrights.cfm

Local HUD Information: www.hud.gov/local/index.cfm?
state=nh
Real Estate Commission: www.nh.gov/nhrec

New Jersey

Consumer Protection: www.njconsumeraffairs.gov/ocp.htm
Disclosures: www.betterhomesnj.com/pdf/
SELLERS_PROPERTY_CONDITION_DISCLOSURE_
STATEMENT.pdf
Fair Housing: www.state.nj.us/dca/fairhousing
Landlord/Tenant Law: www.hud.gov/local/nj/renting/
tenantrights.cfm
Local HUD Infomation: www.hud.gov/local/index.cfm?state=nj
Real Estate Commission: www.state.nj.us/dobi/remnu.shtml

New Mexico

Consumer Protection: www.ago.state.nm.us/divs/cons/cons.htm
Fair Housing: www.sjcounty.net/Dpt/Legal/Ordinances/
Ordinance26.htm.
Landlord/Tenant Law: www.thelpa.com/lpa/
landlord-tenant-law/new-mexico-landlord-tenant-law.html
Local HUD Information: www.hud.gov/local/index.cfm?state=
nm
Real Estate Commission: www.rld.state.nm.us/Real_Estate_
Commission/index.html

New York

Consumer Protection: www.oag.state.ny.us/consumer/consumer_
issues.html

Disclosures: www.dos.state.ny.us/lcns/pdfs/1614.pdf

Fair Housing: www.dhcr.state.ny.us/fheo/fheo.htm

Landlord/Tenant Law: www.hud.gov/local/ny/renting/ tenantrights.
cfm

Local HUD Information: www.hud.gov/local/index.cfm?state=
ny

Office of Real Property Services: www.orps.state.ny.us

Cornell University: http://realestate.cornell.edu

New York University: www.law.nyu.edu/realestatecenter

North Carolina

Consumer Protection: www.ncdoj.com/consumerprotection/
cp_about.jsp

Disclosures: www.ncrec.state.nc.us/forms/rec422.pdf

Fair Housing: www.ncruralcenter.org/guidebook/viewresource.
asp?ID=138

Landlord/Tenant Law: www.hud.gov/local/nc/renting/ tenantrights.
cfm

Local HUD Information: www.hud.gov/local/index.cfm?state=
nc

Real Estate Commission: www.ncrec.state.nc.us/default.html

University of North Carolina: www.kenan-flagler.unc.edu/
KI/realEstate/research.cfm

North Dakota

Consumer Protection: www.ag.state.nd.us/CPAT/CPAT.htm

Fair Housing: www.ndfhc.org

Landlord/Tenant Law: www.hud.gov/local/nd/renting/ tenantrights. cfm

www.ag.state.nd.us/Brochures/FactSheet/TenantRights.pdf

Local HUD Information: www.hud.gov/local/index.cfm?state= nd

Real Estate Commission: www.governor.state.nd.us/boards/ boards-query.asp?Board_ID=93

Ohio

Consumer Protection: www.ag.state.oh.us

Disclosures: www.com.state.oh.us/real/documents/ respropdisclform.eff2007-01-01.pdf

Fair Housing: http://cohhio.org

Foreclosure Prevention Task Force—Governor's Office: www.com.state.oh.us/admn/foreclosure_links.aspx

Landlord/Tenant Law: www.ohiolegalservices.org/OSLSA/ PublicWeb/Library/Index/1690000/1630100/index_html

Local HUD Information: www.hud.gov/local/index.cfm?state= oh

Division of Real Estate and Professional Licensing: www.com.state.oh.us/real

University of Cincinnati: www.business.uc.edu/realestate

Ohio State University: http://fisher.osu.edu/realestate/index.html

Oklahoma

Disclosures: www.okbar.org/obj/articles_04/051504shelton.htm
www.state.ok.us/~orec/news.html

Fair Housing: www.ohc.ok.gov/housing/housing.htm
www.hud.gov/offices/fheo/FHLaws/index.cfm

Landlord/Tenant Law: www.hud.gov/local/ok/renting/ tenantrights.
cfm

Local HUD Information: www.hud.gov/local/index.cfm?state=
ok

Real Estate Commission: www.ok.gov/OREC

Real Estate Contract Form Approved by the Oklahoma Real
Estate Commission:

http://ok.gov/OREC/documents/Uniform%20Contract%20of
%20Sale%20of%20Real%20Estate.(Field)pdf.pdf

Oregon

Consumer Protection: www.doj.state.or.us/finfraud

Disclosures: www.osbar.org/public/legalinfo/1201.htm
www.leg.state.or.us/ors/105.html (you must then scroll down to
105.464)

Fair Housing: www.fhco.org

Landlord/Tenant Law: www.okbar.org/public/brochures/tenbroc.
htm

Local HUD Information: www.hud.gov/local/index.cfm?state=or

Real Estate Agency: www.oregon.gov/REA/index.shtml

Pennsylvania

Consumer Protection: www.attorneygeneral.gov

Disclosures: www.dos.state.pa.us/bpoa/lib/bpoa/20/real_estate_

comm/sellers_property_disclosure_statement.pdf

Fair Housing: www.phrc.state.pa.us

Landlord/Tenant Law: www.hud.gov/local/pa/renting/tenantrights. cfm

Local HUD Information: www.hud.gov/local/index.cfm?state= pa

Real Estate Commission: www.dos.state.pa.us/bpoa/cwp/ view.asp?a=1104&q=433107&papowerNavDLTEST=%7C306 00%7C30609%7C30610%7C

Pennsylvania State University: www.smeal.psu.edu/ires

University of Pennsylvania: http://realestate.wharton.upenn.edu

Puerto Rico

Fair Housing: www.hud.gov/local/pr-vi/working/localpo/fheo.cfm

Local HUD Information: www.hud.gov/local/index.cfm?state= pr-vi

Rhode Island

Consumer Protection: www.riag.state.ri.us/civil/unit.php? name=consumer

Disclosures: www.rilin.state.ri.us/statutes/TITLE5/5-20.8/5-20.8-2.HTM

Fair Housing: www.rifairhousing.org/

Landlord/Tenant Law: www.hud.gov/local/ri/renting/ tenantrights.cfm

Local HUD Information: www.hud.gov/local/index.cfm?state=ri

Real Estate Commmission: www.dbr.state.ri.us/divisions/ commlicensing/realestate.php

South Carolina

Consumer Protection: www.scconsumer.gov

Disclosures: www.llr.state.sc.us/POL/REC/ RECPDF/ DOC360.pdf

Fair Housing: www.state.sc.us/schac/summary_of_the_south_carolina_fa.htm

Landlord/Tenant Law: www.hud.gov/local/sc/renting/tenantrights.cfm

Local HUD Information: www.hud.gov/local/index.cfm?state=sc

Real Estate Commission: www.llr.state.sc.us/POL/REC

University of South Carolina: http://mooreschool.sc.edu/moore/sccre

South Dakota

Consumer Protection: www.state.sd.us/attorney/office/divisions/consumer

Disclosures: http://legis.state.sd.us/statutes/DisplayStatute.aspx?Type=Statute&Statute=43-4-44

Fair Housing: www.ndfhc.org

Landlord/Tenant Law: www.hud.gov/local/sd/renting/tenantrights.cfm

Local HUD Information: www.hud.gov/local/index.cfm?state=sd

Real Estate Commission: www.state.sd.us/sdrec

Tennessee

Consumer Protection: www.state.tn.us/consumer

Disclosures: http://michie.lexisnexis.com/tennessee/lpext.dll?f=templates&fn=main-h.htm&cp=

Fair Housing: www.tennfairhousing.org

Landlord/Tenant Law: www.hud.gov/local/tn/renting/
tenantrights.cfm

Local HUD Information: www.hud.gov/local/index.cfm?state=tn

Real Estate Commission: www.state.tn.us/commerce/boards/trec

Texas

Consumer Protection: www.oag.state.tx.us/consumer/consumer.
shtml

Disclosures: www.trec.state.tx.us/pdf/contracts/OP-H.pdf

Fair Housing: www.twc.state.tx.us/crd/housing_fact.html

Landlord/Tenant Law: http://studentlife.tamu.edu/scrs/sls/
SelfHelp/tenant.htm

Local HUD Information: www.hud.gov/local/index.cfm?state=tx

Southern Methodist University: www.cox.smu.edu/centers/
realestate

Texas A&M: http://recenter.tamu.edu

Utah

Consumer Protection: www.dcp.utah.gov

Fair Housing: www.rules.utah.gov/publicat/code/r608/
r608-001.htm

Landlord/Tenant Law: www.hud.gov/local/ut/renting/tenantrights.
cfm

Local HUD Information: www.hud.gov/local/index.cfm?state=ut

Division of Real Estate: http://realestate.utah.gov

Division of Real Estate–approved Real Estate Purchase Contract:
http://realestate.utah.gov/REForms/New_REPC.pdf

Vermont

Consumer Protection: www.atg.state.vt.us/display.php?smod=8

Disclosures: www.leg.state.vt.us/docs/bills.cfm?Body= S& Session=1996 (scroll down to S.0167)

Fair Housing: www.vtlawhelp.org/Home/PublicWeb/Pages/ Housing/FairHousing

Landlord/Tenant Law: www.leg.state.vt.us/statutes/sections.cfm? Title=09&Chapter=137

Local HUD Information: www.hud.gov/local/index.cfm?state=vt

Real Estate Commission: http://vtprofessionals.org/opr1/ real_estate

Virginia

Consumer Protection: www.oag.state.va.us/CONSUMER/ index.html

Disclosures: www.dpor.virginia.gov/dporweb/reb_consumer.cfm

Fair Housing: www.dpor.virginia.gov/dporweb/fho_overview.cfm

Landlord/Tenant Law: www.hud.gov/local/va/renting/ tenantrights.cfm

Local HUD Information: www.hud.gov/local/index.cfm?state=va

Department of Professional and Occupational Regulation (Real Estate): www.dpor.virginia.gov/dporweb/dpormainwelcome. cfm

Washington, D.C. (*See* District of Columbia)

Washington

Consumer Protection: www.atg.wa.gov/page.aspx?id=1792

Disclosures: http://apps.leg.wa.gov/RCW/default.aspx?cite=64.06

Fair Housing: www.hum.wa.gov/FairHousing/index.htm

Landlord/Tenant Law: www.hud.gov/local/wa/renting/tenantrights.
cfm

Local HUD Information: www.hud.gov/local/index.cfm?state=
wa

Real Estate Commission: www.dol.wa.gov/business/realestate/
realestatecommission.html

Washington State University: www.cb.wsu.edu/~wcrer

West Virginia

Consumer Protection: www.wvago.gov

Disclosures: www.legis.state.wv.us/Bill_Text_HTML/1999_
SESSIONS/RS/BILLS/HB2629%20INTR.htm

Fair Housing: www.wvf.state.wv.us/wvhrc/index.htm

Landlord/Tenant Law: www.legis.state.wv.us/WVCODE/37/
masterfrmFrm.htm (scroll to 37-6-1 and subsequent sections.)

Local HUD Information: www.hud.gov/local/index.cfm?state=
wv

Real Estate Commission: www.wvrec.org

Wisconsin

Consumer Protection: www.wisconsin.gov/state/app/consumer?
COMMAND=gov.wi.state.cpp.consumer.command.
LoadConsumerHome

Disclosures: www.wisbar.org/am/template.cfm?section=wisconsin
_lawyer&template=/cm/contentdisplay.cfm&contentid=49518
www.legis.state.wi.us/statutes/Stat0709.pdf

Fair Housing: www.fairhousingwisconsin.com/Laws_and_
Remedies.htm

Landlord/Tenant Law: www.hud.gov/local/wi/renting/tenantrights.

cfm

Local HUD Information: www.hud.gov/local/index.cfm?state= wi

Department of Regulation and Licensing (Real Estate Broker, Salesperson, and Apprentice): http://drl.wi.gov/prof/burbiz. htm

Wisconsin, University of www.bus.wisc.edu/wcre/

Wyoming

Consumer Protection: http://attorneygeneral.state.wy.us/consumer. htm

Disclosures: http://legisweb.state.wy.us/2007/Summaries/HB0274. htm

Fair Housing: http://legisweb.state.wy.us/2005/Introduced/HB0267. pdf

Landlord/Tenant Law: www.hud.gov/local/wy/renting/tenantrights. cfm

Local HUD Information: www.hud.gov/local/index.cfm? state= wy

Real Estate Commission: http://realestate.state.wy.us

Index

About the Author

Denise L. Evans received her law degree from the University of Alabama Law School, with a concentration in real estate, tax, and finance. While a law student, she served on the Board of Editors for the Journal of the Legal Profession, published two scholarly articles, was Director of the Legal Research Department, and clerked with a law firm that had a large real estate practice. She graduated at the top of her class, earning the prestigious Henderson M. Somerville Prize. Afterward, she spent several years in Houston, Texas, in commercial litigation, much of it related to real estate. At the pinnacle of her legal career, she headed a specialized department of eight litigation attorneys and support staff, and conducted legal training for lawyers throughout southern Texas.

Today, she is a successful businesswoman in a variety of real estate–related businesses, including one that she sold several years ago for a profit of several million dollars. She is a licensed commercial real estate broker with a very active practice. She has twenty years of experience in conducting seminars, consulting, and passing on her secrets and insights to other people, as well as successfully implementing them herself.

She resides with her husband, two Chinese Pugs, a German Shepherd, half a million honeybees (really!), and assorted wildlife on forty acres of relatively blissful peace on Lake Tuscaloosa, in Alabama.